CONVERTED TO CHRIST THROUGH THE BOOK OF MORMON

EDITED BY
EUGENE ENGLAND

Deseret Book Company
Salt Lake City, Utah

For Ezra Taft Benson
Our Book of Mormon Prophet

Library of Congress Cataloging-in-Publication Data

Converted to Christ through the Book of Mormon / edited by
Eugene England.

    p. cm.

  Includes index.

  ISBN 0-87579-268-5

  1. Converts, Mormon—Biography.   2. Book of Mormon—Devotional
use.   I. England, Eugene.

BX8693.C66   1989

289.3'22—dc20   89-36275

                                                 CIP

Printed in the United States of America

10   9   8   7   6   5   4   3   2   1

CONTENTS

INTRODUCTION

THE SPIRIT OF CHRIST COMES FROM EVERY PAGE

EUGENE ENGLAND
Provo, Utah

I had my "reconversion" to the Book of Mormon (to use the word I have chosen for the experiences of life-long Mormons) when I was a missionary in Hawaii in 1956. Yes, I had read the book and studied passages for talks, but I had not been brought to Christ by it.

Near the end of my mission (Charlotte and I had been called to Samoa together right after our marriage and transferred to Hawaii for our first child's birth, then she had gone home), I faced the most difficult spiritual challenge of my life to that point. A man we were teaching on the island of Maui had come to believe the gospel was true, but he couldn't find the strength to repent. He would make promises to change his ways, to get rid of habits very harmful to himself and his family, but he would break his promises and then suffer terribly from guilt. He felt ashamed, not good enough for Christ, and too weak to become good.

We tried all kinds of ways to help him be strong, from telling him about the hell he was making for himself and about the heaven with his family he was destroying, to hourly calls to check up on him, to going over and over the logical "steps" of repentance. Nothing worked, and his family, who had joined the Church, and we missionaries were all near despair. Then I remembered Joseph Smith's claim that the Book of Mormon was "the most correct book" in the world and that its principles provided the best way to get near to God. (*Teachings of the*

1

Prophet Joseph Smith, sel. Joseph Fielding Smith [Salt Lake City: Deseret Book, 1938], p. 194.)

I studied the Book of Mormon, looking for ways to help our friend. As I did, I went back over my notes from Lowell Bennion's institute classes, which I remembered had stressed the new vision of salvation through Christ's atonement given by the Book of Mormon. Slowly I found again the key I had been taught but which had not meant enough until now when it was needed so badly. Then we read the main passages about Christ from the Book of Mormon with our friend, and he felt the spirit of complete love from his Savior. I remember when we came to the sermon of Amulek, in Alma 34, where he teaches that the suffering of Christ brings about the bowels of mercy, enough to break through the bands of justice and give us the means to have enough faith to repent. This was exactly what our friend needed—and as he read the Book of Mormon passages he finally understood and *felt* it and thus was able to accept Christ's love and repent. I believe his wife's love, never critical, always encouraging (and our own struggling efforts to be like her) played some role. But the turning point was when he felt love from Christ, conveyed by the promises and spirit of the Book of Mormon. He said, "If Christ can have this kind of love for me, who am I to refuse to accept it—and not accept myself." With this new strength, he became a new person, almost overnight.

My own life didn't change as much, but I saw clearly then that the Book of Mormon had the best answer to the chief human question, "What can we do about our sins?" and that it also contained the best direct help to actually bring people to repent. My sense of Christ's atoning love that began there on Maui has become central to my own efforts to change, to my way of seeing literature and politics and human violence and healing, and to my efforts to counsel people.

Once, when I was bishop of a married student ward at Brigham Young University, one of the ward members asked me to talk with a friend who had tried suicide and was often terribly depressed. As we met, I quickly found that, like many young Latter-day Saints I had counseled, she had a strong sense of justice and self-condemnation but a very weak sense of Christ's mercy and love. She spoke quickly and harshly about her failings and her despair. I felt I should not talk but simply read with her, from the Book of Mormon, those passages that teach the Atonement and convey its spirit. After a while peace visibly came over her and she began to weep, and when she left she had been helped.

The Book of Mormon is the unique tangible witness in the world of the most important intangible reality, the love of Christ and His power to heal and save us. I feel this power, after many readings and much study, whenever I turn to any part of the book. I immediately am brought close to tears by the Spirit of Christ that comes from every page. We who have felt that tangible power in various ways — like electricity, or with burning that is a fire in the bones or that fills the body, or through the way the book physically calls attention to itself or seems to be able to affect its environment — use quite similar language in our descriptions, whether we are from Barbados or Hungary or Utah, whether college professors or cowpunchers. That power serves a great variety of purposes — to prepare a boy like John Harrington to receive the gospel many years later, to give a teenager like Donna Chase the courage to turn directly to Christ despite the real costs, to provide rock-bottom conviction for otherwise quite skeptical scholars like William A. Wilson and David Whittaker. Yet not everyone seems to need such physical evidence. Like Dustin Heuston and Merrill Bradshaw, they come, through long study, to a solid conviction that is finally confirmed emotionally. The letters and narratives in this volume provide a great panorama of the many fascinating ways the Book of Mormon is leading new converts to Christ and reconverting life-long members all over the world.

What a remarkable book! More than 35 million in eighty languages have been printed, and the pace is accelerating: 1.2

million in 1984 and 3.4 million in 1988. At this rate at least
another 35 million will be published in just the next ten years.
The Book of Mormon is now, next to the Bible and the Koran,
probably the book read most widely—by more people in more
places—in the world. Each year hundreds of thousands of
people, from Argentinians, Bostonians, and Californians to Zulus, from children and new converts and prospective elders
to middle-aged cultural Mormons and older couples going on
missions, have their lives dramatically changed by reading the
book and responding to its power. As the witnesses in this
collection demonstrate, that power is manifest in ways that fit
the unique ways and circumstances and language of each person, but it always brings meekness and lowliness of heart,
sorrow for sin but strength to repent, and courage to act and
speak in entirely new ways. In other words, it always leads
people to Christ—to accept Him as both judge and friend and
to follow His command, in the book, to be like Him.

My father is a good example of a reconversion. He was
raised in a Mormon village, Moreland, Idaho, by goodly Mormon parents, but it wasn't until he left home at seventeen for
a job in a Union Pacific paintshop in Pocatello and read the
Book of Mormon before work each morning that he came to
know the Savior. During that time, he had a dream in which
Christ came to him and told him He loved and accepted him.
It is clear, as he tells me this again nearly seventy years later,
that he can still feel that first presence of grace. It led him to
change his life in many ways, large and small: to go on a mission
instead of becoming an airline pilot, to marry my mother because the same Being brought her to him by the hand in a
later dream, and especially to feel what I call the "Spirit of
Lehi," a continuing determination to help fulfill the great Book
of Mormon promises to the descendants of Lehi.

My father and mother, influenced by the "Spirit of Lehi,"
gradually came to the conviction that they must consecrate all
their surplus to help take the gospel to Lehi's descendants, in
North and South America and Polynesia. And through their

consecration of time as well as means, and their sensitivity to the Spirit, they were in a position to help directly with the development of what is now the most dramatic way the Book of Mormon is going out to the world, the Family to Family Program. In 1969 my father was working with William Bradshaw as a host at the Temple Square Visitors' Center and with him occasionally giving out somewhat personalized copies of the Book of Mormon to people with special interest. Then Arlene Crawley, from Kaysville, told Brother Bradshaw and my father about her Primary class project, which led the three of them to create the family-to-family approach of sending copies of the Book of Mormon on missions all over the world and eventually to build the project into an approved, accelerating, Churchwide program.

Sister Crawley tells of the inspiration and struggles of those first efforts and how the Lord works, sometimes with an amazing variety of imperfect people, to achieve his purposes. Her story leaves off with Brother Bradshaw's successful trip in the fall of 1970 to teach the program to mission presidents in South America, a trip that he made more extensive at Sister Crawley's urging. I can confirm her conjecture that it was my father who helped donate the five hundred books that made that seeding effort possible, because he asked me and my sister Ann to provide some of them. I have letters from Brazil written in the spring of 1971 by people who received the books given by my own family and copies of the answers we wrote.

Those treasured letters show, even at that early stage, the effectiveness of Sister Crawley's inspired idea that a personal testimony and picture in a Book of Mormon, with an invitation to correspond, is a way every member can directly respond to President David O. McKay's challenge to be a missionary. Some wrote back while they were still investigating, in gratitude and efforts toward friendship: "It becomes more and more difficult these days to find people like you, concerning yourselves with your fellowman even at this great distance. For this reason I've a great admiration for you and this gesture of felicitation with your fellowman." (Zilmar de Moraes, Canoas, Brazil.) Some were genuinely interested in the book and clearly on their way to conversion: "I read part of the book after [the sisters] left and was very impressed. I found the concepts of the book very profound, also an idea I had never encountered before, Christ in America." (Romullo Ferro, Pelotas, Brazil.)

We wrote back long letters of explanation and testimony about the gospel and the Church and helped our children write the children in the families. The missionaries, who provided the translations, often wrote notes of thanks, commenting on how effective the new program was compared to their previous efforts. I recently received a letter from a former student who had gone to Brazil on a mission and found one of those nineteen-year-old copies of the Book of Mormon, with our picture and testimony in it, in the home of what is now a stalwart Mormon family.

After Dad and Brother Bradshaw, working eventually with President Spencer W. Kimball, got approval for implementing the program Churchwide, Brother Bradshaw oversaw it for about eight years from his office in the Visitors' Center, while gradually members throughout the Church became involved through yearly drives in the priesthood quorums. Then in 1982 the program was moved into its own building, the old Lafayette School north of the Church Office Building, and was directed by two Church service missionary couples, Helen and Ray Hunter Barton, Jr., and Virgil and Audrey Peterson. When I talked with them in 1984, the number of books they were sending out had increased from 3000 a month to about 15,000 copies a month, and they were receiving increasingly enthusiastic reports of success from all over the world. The expanding program was moved into the larger Church Exhibits Building on Fourth North in 1985. Robert and Enid Burton were put in charge, and Ferrell and Blanch McGhie were appointed in 1986. The numbers of books sent out continued to grow, dramatically spurred by the addresses of President Ezra Taft Benson and, I believe, the "Spirit of Lehi," which seemed gradually to invest the whole Church as a result: 447,000 in 1986; 917,000 in 1987; 1,413,000 in 1988; and 1,200,00 in just the first half of 1989. Especially has that spirit been felt since the October 1988 general conference, in which President Benson made a dramatic appeal to "move the Book of Mormon forward now in a marvelous manner" and prophesied that it would flood the earth with millions of copies. The response of people in buying copies to be sent has been so great that the Church has now placed the program under a full-time professional, Brother L. Jay Monk of the Missionary Department, who is assisted by an advisory committee composed of the Bartons, the Petersons, the McGhies, and LaVorn and Bea Sparks. The staff has grown from 4 Church Service missionaries in 1982 to 169, and the program is expanding beyond the huge Exhibits Building.

Besides the many of us who can do our part each month by contributing through our ward or branch family-to-family project, individuals throughout the Church are being touched by the "Spirit of Lehi" in ways that impel them to unusual efforts. My father interested his friends Vadna and G. Albin Matson in the program, and they have sent many copies each year since the mid seventies, receiving letters from grateful converts from many nations. Margaret and Stanley Kimball, of St. George, Utah, have sent out more than twenty thousand copies and, from letters from converts and missionaries, they know of more than thirteen hundred people converted through those books. In the first half of December 1988, they learned of twelve baptisms, from Spain, El Salvador, Bolivia, Argentina, Hawaii, and Mexico. And many others are feeling what President Benson in October 1988 general conference called "this burden" and also "this blessing which [God] has placed on the whole Church." (*Ensign*, Nov. 1988, p. 6.)

I felt the pull of the "Spirit of Lehi" when I heard President Benson in that conference challenge "our Church writers, teachers, and leaders to tell us more Book of Mormon conversion stories that will strengthen our faith and prepare great missionaries." My heart responded especially to his call to "let us know how it [the Book of Mormon] leads us to Christ." (P. 5.) This book is the result of that challenge. I am grateful to Deseret Book for accepting and acting on my proposal so quickly and for the fine cooperation of mission presidents, friends, and colleagues all over the world — and especially the many people who made the effort to write and tell their own stories. For some it was a first effort and very difficult. For all it was a challenge to share sacred personal experiences in print.

I have done everything I could to respect the personal nature and sacredness of these testimonies. I have chosen the stories printed from the many I received to show the great variety of people being brought to Christ by this other testament and also to capture the remarkable similarity of experiences the book has brought over time and place, from Parley P. Pratt to the latest convert, and from India to Idaho. I believe you can hear the varied but amazingly consistent voice of the contemporary kingdom of God in these stories. I trust that you will indeed be strengthened in your own faith by them and led to know the book better for yourself and to be a better missionary with it. I especially hope that you too will be converted to Christ in new ways.

FAMILY TO FAMILY

This section begins with the story of the beginnings of what may now be the most dramatically expanding program of the Church and probably the most effective single proselyting technique. Arlene Crawley tells how she was inspired to help her family and her Primary class begin "sending the Book of Mormon on a mission" twenty years ago and how the program developed at the Salt Lake Temple Visitors' Center. Then there is a sampling of letters from people all over the world to those who are now sending their pictures and testimonies in the Family to Family Program.

Another burgeoning family effort is the calling of older couples as missionaries, and a powerful family to family effort since Samuel Smith took the first copies of the Book of Mormon to neighbors around Palmyra is the sharing of the book with friends and family. The Hawkinses and the Jensens tell of their use of the Book of Mormon to teach the gospel in South Africa and Wales. Then John Daniel and Noel Owen tell of their conversion through copies of the Book of Mormon given them by Mormon friends, and Mark Rasmussen and Dorothy Watkins tell about conversion through copies provided through the efforts of members of their own families. Danuta Mandziak writes of the missionary couple who gave her the Book of Mormon and baptized her in Poland, and finally, Barbara Kovalenko tells of a new opening for the Book of Mormon through a family visit to Russia.

THE BEGINNINGS OF
THE FAMILY TO FAMILY PROGRAM

ARLENE CRAWLEY
Kaysville, Utah

In the summer of 1969, our family decided that the Book of
Mormon was our favorite scripture. We had taught our children
that not everyone had these wonderful scriptures to teach their
families about Jesus' coming to the Americas. We decided to
ask Heavenly Father how we might share the Book of Mormon
with friends and others throughout the world without pushing
our religion on them. Most of the non-Mormon families we
knew had just had new babies, so we made something for each
baby to send along with a Book of Mormon. If the family didn't
have a baby but had children, we planned to give them "quiet
books" that I had made in Relief Society.

Each of us wanted to send a book, so we set up extra chores
to do to earn our own money. We chose five families we knew
in the States, one for each of us. After our money was earned,
we purchased our copies of the Book of Mormon and took
them home. We wrote inside the cover, telling each family we
wanted them to have a gift of love and the greatest gift we
could give them was the restored gospel of Jesus Christ. We
then gift wrapped the books and the baby gifts and wrote letters
to the missionaries about our friends so that they might be
more effective in teaching them the gospel. We didn't have the
addresses of the missions, so my husband and I went to the
Church Offices to see if the missionaries could deliver the
books and the gifts and possibly make a return visit to discuss
the Book of Mormon.

Everyone we talked to seemed interested but didn't know
if what we wanted to do was according to Church policy or
not. They referred us to Ned Winder of the Missionary Department. We had a delightful conversation with him, and he
obtained the names of the mission presidents and their ad-

dresses. He liked the idea that we were writing to the missionaries and sending a door opener for them.

We asked Brother Winder if he knew of any pamphlets — besides the Joseph Smith Story, which we had — that we might send along with the Book of Mormon to further interest our friends. He suggested several and directed us to the lower level of the Visitors' Center at Temple Square. He told us that we would find all we were looking for there.

From behind the counter on the lower level of the Visitors' Center emerged a man with the most heartwarming smile and the warmest handshake we had ever received. His name was William Bradshaw. We asked him for the pamphlets, and he hesitated to gather them for the moment, wanting to know more. We showed him an envelope containing a Book of Mormon, a baby gift, and the letter to the missionaries. He smiled and said that for about two years he and his friend Eugene England, Sr., both hosts at the Visitors' Center, had been handing out copies of the Book of Mormon to people really interested in reading it. The books had been purchased by individual Church members to give out at the Center.

Brother Bradshaw pulled three books from under the counter. He asked us to see what was different about them. The cover was the same, the text was the same, and the pictures were the same. Then he told us to open the book as if we were going to read it. Inside the cover of the first book was pasted a typewritten statement of four things that make a balanced life. There was no name or address in this book. In the second book was a typewritten sheet with Brother Bradshaw's name and address on it, statements from the Book of Mormon and their location, and encouragement to read of the book's truth for a happy life. In the third book was the picture of an eight-year-old boy from Jordan, Utah. Underneath it he had printed his name and address. An envelope with the sender's name and address and two sheets of paper were in each book.

I was really taken by the book with the boy's picture in it and asked Brother Bradshaw about it. "We want to include every member in the Church in missionary work who wants to help us out here at the Center," he said, "and this little boy thought he was too young to write his testimony, so he put his picture in the book." We were so excited by all that Brother Bradshaw had to say that we stayed two hours, listening to him. Before we left, we promised we would return with some books from our family. His enthusiasm and encouragement were really catching.

We decided to go to the Distribution Center on Richards Street to get other pamphlets. As we looked around there, we found some wallet-sized cards with President David O. McKay's picture on them and a message that read, "God help us to fulfill our responsibility to our callings, and especially our responsibility of bringing the glad tidings of the gospel to our friends and neighbors, and every member a missionary." At that moment my whole being was filled with warmth and joy. I could hardly wait to get home to prepare a poster to show our children what we were going to be doing as a family.

I just finished the finishing touches on the poster when the children walked in from school. It read, "Let's send the [I placed there a picture of the Book of Mormon] on a mission. It costs only [I pasted on two large pictures of quarters] to bring happiness to others," and there I pasted on a picture of a family. The children were really excited about continuing to be missionaries. Right away we asked a neighbor to use a whole roll of film taking pictures of our family holding up our poster and the Book of Mormon. Once again we set up extra chores for each of us to do to earn the money to send the Book of Mormon on a mission. We decided we would send two books apiece and have them ready in two weeks to take to Brother Bradshaw to hand out at the Visitors' Center.

After the children were settled in their beds, I took out my Primary manual to start preparing the next lesson. I sat on the couch and spread out my things. There were the cards with the picture of President McKay on them. Suddenly I knew how I could teach my Primary children to help others learn about

Heavenly Father. We could send the Book of Mormon on a mission! With great excitement and speed I prepared two posters. The first poster was like the one I had prepared for my own children. The second poster read, "WE SENT THE BOOK OF MORMON ON A MISSION AND BECAME 'EVERY MEMBER A MISSIONARY.' "

At Primary I asked the children if they wanted to learn about becoming missionaries right now and bringing the love of the gospel of Jesus Christ to their brothers and sisters in the world. They all said they did and grew really excited. This was their opportunity to help the missionaries who were older get into homes to teach the gospel of Jesus Christ to people who really wanted to know the truth, which had been restored to the earth through our modern day prophet, Joseph Smith. I told them that they were to do something extra to earn the money to buy a book.

The next Primary day was a special one. I had books ready for the class members to purchase. I wondered if every child would remember and I thought about calling to remind them, but then I decided to see if they would remember on their own. As the children entered Primary, they had grins on their faces that wouldn't quit, and they all held their coins tightly in their hands.

I couldn't sleep that night, waiting to take the books to Brother Bradshaw at the Visitors' Center. He knew our family had planned on doing the project but didn't know that the Spirit had inspired me to include the Primary children in the project. It seemed the night would never end, but finally the morning came. When I arrived at the center and Brother Bradshaw saw me, the biggest smile spread across his face. I waited while he taught an investigator. Oh, how I wish I could be a part of this work, I thought. When he was finished, I took the books out of my bag and laid them on the counter. He was dumbfounded when he found out that every one of the children in my Primary class, including the little girl who had never attended Primary before, had participated. He promised that these books would go to someone special.

That afternoon when school was over, almost every child came to my home to see if the books had been delivered to the Visitor's Center and if they were on their way to their mission. I assured them that the books were indeed on their way and that Brother Bradshaw was thrilled that they wanted to be missionaries. I told them they were the first children in the Church to "send the Book of Mormon on a mission" in Primary, and he was very proud of them.

Only three of the children received letters back, but the others felt that the letters were theirs too because we shared them. I told the children never to give up praying for their books to go to someone who would be guided by the Holy Ghost to know the truth of the Book of Mormon. I gave the same lesson to my children because they were anxious about not having received missionary letters, either. After April 1970 general conference, we received the first letter (for Scott Harris), and soon the other two children (Tom Allen and Mary Hawkins) received letters. Easter was a nice time of year to receive letters about the Book of Mormon.

Dear Scott,

During my visit to Salt Lake City early this month, I spoke with Brother William W. Bradshaw at the Visitors' Center. Brother Bradshaw told me about the "Special Delivery Referral Program," and he handed me a Book of Mormon containing your picture and your name and address.

I visited Salt Lake City because of Conference. I am the first Counselor of President Paul J. Jonkees, who is the president of the Holland Stake in the Netherlands Mission and I have asked them to find a nonmember boy about your age, hand him your Book of Mormon, and ask him to write you a letter. The missionaries promised to do their utmost to find a family in which is a boy who may become your pen friend. So, you see, "Special Delivery" has already become a challenge for the missionaries. You can see how it might work out. I will ask the missionaries how they are getting on by and by. . . .

Carl Schulders
Dordrecht, Netherlands

Dear Brother Harris,   May 17, 1970

A few weeks ago we received your Book of Mormon from Brother Schulders. He asked us to find a young person who was interested in reading the Book of Mormon in English, and to give it to the person as a gift from you.

We are very pleased to tell you that we have placed your Book of Mormon with a young lady about 10 years old. Her whole family is investigating the Church right now. This young lady speaks very good English because she and her family lived in Australia for a number of years. She was very excited about writing a letter to you.

It's really great to see that you are doing your part in following the challenge of President McKay, who asked that every member be a missionary. I know that through our efforts this is really going to help this family accept the gospel. . . .

Elder David Ray Cope and Elder John C. Gobel

Before Brother Bradshaw's death in the summer of 1987, he contacted the brethren in Holland about the family the Book of Mormon went to from Scott Harris. He learned that the family had joined the Church and was active. What a great missionary this little seven-year-old boy was. It must bring joy to his heart and to the heart of his family.

In the fall of 1970 we moved to Roy, Utah. When we were invited to speak in church the first month, I presented our Book of Mormon program to the ward. I took my camera, and after the meeting I took several pictures of the members and their families. The bishop invited Brother Bradshaw to come to our ward to tell more about it. Brother Bradshaw was well received, and many ward members participated directly with him in "sending the Book of Mormon on a mission." Brother Bradshaw soon picked up that saying of mine instead of his "Special Delivery Referral Program." I don't think he even realized he changed the name.

When I first began working with Brother Bradshaw, he was only handing out copies of the Book of Mormon at the Visitors' Center unless someone asked him to mail a copy to a relative in the mission field. I suggested to him that we mail books to people in the mission field, just as we were mailing them to our friends. Brother Ned Winder gave me a list of mission presidents for us to use in this project. Brother Bradshaw gave me two sample testimonies and asked me to work out something. I put all our ideas together, including the testimonies of the children, because I felt the books would thus have more meaning to the receivers. The result was that a picture of a family was pasted above their testimony on the inside front cover. This was our family's message:

Our family is happy as we send to you our gift of love and truth. The Book of Mormon is a history of the people on the American continents. It testifies that Jesus Christ visited the Americas and gave the same commandments and healed the sick as he did on the old continent. It stands together with the Bible as a second witness that God lives, that Jesus Christ, His Son, leads and guides His church. We testify to you that the Book of Mormon is the word of God. We encourage you to gather as a family and read from the Book of Mormon and pray and ask God if it is true.

If you have a sincere heart, He will reveal the truth to you through the Holy Ghost.

Please write to our family.

Love from your new friends,
The Crawley Family

The project began to grow. Instead of five to twenty books being given out at the Visitors' Center each month, we were sending out hundreds a month to the missions. Brother Bradshaw was always in demand as a speaker to present the program, and he always went at his own expense. In the fall of 1970 he decided to go to South America to be with his daughter when she had her baby, and he hoped to present the program to the Saints in Paraguay. I asked him if he was stopping in Saõ Paulo, Brazil, where Sherman and Jo Ann Hibbert presided, and he said he changed planes there. "Brother Bradshaw," I said, "I am sending you on a mission to Saõ Paulo, Brazil."

He looked at me and said, "What?"

I reminded him that we had met because we were sending baby gifts with copies of the Book of Mormon to our non-member friends so they could learn how to have their family forever. "So," I said, "I am sending copies of the Book of Mormon on a mission with you to Saõ Paulo to the Hibberts, along with a gift for their new baby." I told him that my family and I wanted to send one hundred books, but we couldn't come up with enough money. Within a very short time, someone donated enough money so we could send one hundred books. To this day I think it was Brother Eugene England, Sr., although no one has ever told me so.

I asked Brother Bradshaw to take at least five hundred books to Brazil because the Hibberts would need that many. He looked at me strangely, and I said, "You don't know the Hibberts. They are just like you, and they know a good tool for teaching the gospel when they see it, so go prepared." I don't think Brother Bradshaw planned on taking anywhere near that many books when he first planned to go, but several large donations made it possible for him to take that many.

Brother Bradshaw told me later that when he got to Brazil, President Hibbert felt impressed by the Spirit to invite him to go to the mission presidents' conference in Quito, Ecuador, to present the program to the mission presidents. They rode sitting up on a rickety old bus all day and all night without any sleep. At first, Elder Gordon B. Hinckley, who was presiding, reproved President Hibbert for inviting Brother Bradshaw to the conference, but Elder Hinckley responded to the promptings of the Spirit to allow Brother Bradshaw time to speak. Brother Bradshaw spoke for an hour, and when he was finished, President Hinckley stood and asked the mission presidents how many copies of the Book of Mormon each wanted. Most of the books Brother Bradshaw had with him went to Chile, where they have brought many converts to the Church. In November and December 1970, the Hibberts reported, 28 percent of the baptisms in their mission in Brazil came from the "Send the Book of Mormon on a Mission" program.

Brother England tried for years to get the program approved for Churchwide use. He did not give up on the project, though he was told the Church was not yet ready for it. Finally he spoke with Elder Spencer W. Kimball, who was then head of the Missionary Committee, and showed him the posters I had made to teach my family and my Primary class, as well as the poster I had made for Brother Bradshaw to take to South America to teach the Saints. This poster was also used to get visitors and guides at the Visitors' Center to join in. On green felt, lovely gold lettering declared, "Every Member a Missionary—By Sending the Book of Mormon on a Mission," and pictures of my thirteen CTR Pilots were arranged on the poster. Elder Kimball looked at the pictures of the Primary children and saw the great happiness and love on their faces. He said that the program would eventually be implemented in the Church, and when he became President, it was.

In 1975, Brother England telephoned to invite my husband and me and our children to the Visitors' Center. There we watched a group of missionaries from the Mission Home learn about the program. The missionaries were given complete instructions, two free copies of the Book of Mormon, and the incentive that if they placed one copy with someone who was later baptized, they would receive a whole box of copies of the Book of Mormon with testimonies in them to give away.

Then Brother England gave us the wonderful news that the project we had helped start, "Send the Book of Mormon on a Mission," was now a Churchwide program.

I Would Like to Thank You
for the Goodness

Dear Reeder Family,   December 1, 1988

It's my greatest pleasure to thank you sincerely with all my heart for making it possible for me to receive the Book of Mormon. I believe God will bless you more abundantly for a good job done.

As I read the Bible, I felt joy and peace within my soul, and that was a clear testimony that the book is true, and I believed the Book of Mormon instantly.

I have been baptized with the Spirit since yesterday, 30-11-88, and I was blessed by the president of the church in Zurich, Switzerland, so I am now a member of your church.

I would also like to thank you once again, for the goodness. I always pray and ask God to keep you and bless you in all the days of your life. Amen.

Kenneth Ofosu Gyan
Lucerne, Switzerland

Craig, Phyllis & Trisha Harward,   October 17, 1988

I am twenty-one years old and I have had the great fortune to have met two missionaries from The Church of Jesus Christ of Latter-day Saints.

With their help, the help of the whole church here in Ottawa, the help from the Lord in answering all my prayers and questions, and also the help you have given in providing for me a copy of the Book of Mormon, I have begun to realize that it is full of truth and it defines the only true way to live my life in greater service to God.

Already I have experienced some of the wonderful blessings of The Church of Jesus Christ of Latter-day Saints and I look forward to learning, developing and experiencing more of the joys in my many years to come.

My baptism is going to be taking place on the 20th of October. (It will probably have happened before you receive this.)

I would like to hear from you about your experiences and joys both in and outside of the Church. It makes me happy to see and hear of all the wonderful people who are truly my brothers and sisters.

Robert M. Gagnon
Ottawa, Ontario, Canada

Dear Howard and Stella,   March 24, 1988

I am reading in the Book of Mormon. I think it is great. Sister Larsen and Sister Holt are teaching me fantastic things. I really like reading the Book of Mormon. Thank you for sending the copy. I am going to be baptized April 10th and going to watch conference. I asked God if I should join the Mormon church and He said yes.

Rita Stivison
Logan, Ohio

Dear Sister in Christ—   May 25, 1988

Permit me to express my most sincere thanks for the gift of a Book of Mormon, which you have offered me. For me it is an opportunity to thank you again for the service you have rendered me. May God bless you and your whole family, may he accord you a long life, happiness and joy, and may He continue to inspire you that you can be in Him and His Son, Jesus Christ.

In being your brother in Jesus Christ, I hold the Priesthood of Aaron and am an instructor in the Primary.

I would like it if we could correspond more so we could become acquainted with each other's culture in spite of the distance which separates us. Praise be to our Lord for His goodness (Joshua 1:8–9) and for His prophet, Joseph Smith, and for His Church of Jesus Christ of Latter-day Saints.

Tshipepele-Kande
Kinshasa, Zaire, Africa
(Translated by David and Helen Wright)

Dear Brother and Sister Kimball,   March 10, 1988

My name is Amelia Esther and I have three children. My son Paulo Heber also accepted to be baptized on the same day as I. That was December 19, 1987. I was a person in search of the true church and prayed always, asking Heavenly Father that something good happen or that He open a door in that our Lord accept me like I am for with the help of the members of the Church to help me overcome some faults that don't satisfy the Lord. And it happened that on the 3rd of November, 1987, I could receive in my house two missionaries, Sister Lehi and Sister Sandra that erred correctly. Erred, because without their knowledge they left their area and it was in that way that it happened. And today I feel happy and very thankful for the Book of Mormon that they left so that I could study, and today with much love I thank you for the great present that you sent and that our Lord sent in my house. Today I look to perfect myself, searching always that which is of the will of the Lord. Only I can ask and I can thank, in the name of the Lord, to bless you for giving me this honor that is to be brothers and sisters in Jesus Christ.

Amelia Esther Ywagatuma
Londrina, Paraná, Brazil

My name is Paulo Heber. Like my mother said [above], we are thankful for the Holy Ghost and to have received baptism. I didn't think two times to be baptized because I felt really that that was the path [I was already on].

In that manner, Heavenly Father was blessing me with the paths of the Holy Ghost.

Well, I stay very thankful and emotional when I received a level of the Aaronic Priesthood and more when I was invited to be the 2nd counselor and secretary in the presidency of the Young Men, for this I am able to give classes to the deacons.

I stop here and thank you for having given the Book of Mormon so our knowledge can enlarge. I wait in this way for your response. Much thanks!

Paulo Heber Ywagatuma
(Translated by Helene Leli)

Mr. Kimball & family,

I am writing to you to say thank you for your gift of the Book of Mormon. It has given me so much in so little time. It has given me a new way of life. I really owe you so very much, and one day I hope to meet you so I can say thank you face to face.

Still I am hoping to come over some time next year to see the temple. I have heard so much it about from the missionaries so maybe we could meet and you could take me to one of the churches over there. Anyway, one bit of good news. I had my baptism on Christmas Day and it was really wonderful and this is all thanks to you and the missionaries.

Michelle Gratton
Pitsea, Essex, England

Dear Mr. Stanley C. Kimball,   November 16, 1986

I have received two of your donated books plus 121 more donated books, all of which I've given out with a clear, plain, understandable explanation of them. I'm in prison, I converted in here when I was reading the Book of Mormon. I really believed it, my mother gave it to me on a visit. She's Greek Orthodox.

I believed so much I requested visits from the missionaries, Elders Cronerman, Coy, Doxey, Strater, Warburton, Stone, Daskibakis, Day, Norton, all over the period of a year while I was in the city jail. . . . My lifetime goal is 10,000 Books of Mormon passed out. So far I've read the Book of Mormon 1 1/2 times and I am still listening to the President of the Church making it the center of his teaching. Right now I trying to buy *The History of the Church of Jesus Christ*. They cost $15.95 a volume for eight volumes. So far I've saved $95 from prison earnings and need $40 more to cover the tax and postage. Then I can read the history. As a nonmember I intend to follow the gospel as a member would. It will be six and 2/3 years before I can join the Church because of parole but I am hoping they'll let me on parole in 21 months God willing. . . .

With love I do write this letter mostly to say thanks for setting such a fine example of true faith. I will some day be with my brothers and going on a mission and doing temple work and marry my sweetheart forever and our children will be with us. In the name of my Savior Jesus Christ.

Demetrius Athemasopoulos
Astoria, New York

Mme. Rigby—   21 June 1988

Since 1985 I have been completely off balance (unemployed, disordered home life for lack of means). I began to despair of my life on earth and that of my children. I have five daughters and five sons who are scattered. A nephew who lives with me prevailed upon me to read the brochures of The Church of Jesus Christ of Latter-day Saints. He succeeded in interesting me in taking the discussions with the missionaries. I have had two lessons and have reread Mormon 10:1–34 and 1 Nephi 11:1–41.

I understand that God asks three things in order for us to have His mercy and stop our sins: (1) faith in Christ, (2) hope, and (3) charity. We must repent, believe in the Holy Trinity and be baptized in His name.

For myself, I feel more and more relaxed. I hope that I will become employed permanently before long and that other problems will disappear. I will bless God always and especially awaiting my baptism. I continue reading my Book of Mormon. I am forty-eight years old.

Mutamba Kambala Tshisekedi
Kinshasa, Zaire, Africa
(Translated by David and Helen Wright)

Dear Friend Nelly:

It is with great pleasure that I write you. Even though I don't know you personally, I feel in my heart that I really do know you as a marvelous person! I would like to thank you for the great present you have given me, the Book of Mormon. After reading this book a few times, and also praying, I began to feel nearer to my Father in Heaven and Jesus Christ, and began to feel great peace and joy in my heart. I am happy to say that the words in this book are true, just like the Bible is too. The words of the book seem completely natural, they bloom, flow, shine, cry and laugh.

Thank you very much from the bottom of my heart for this great book. I will keep its words with much love and respect in my heart.

Ana Maria Alves de Meira
Ponta Gressa, Brazil

Dear ———————,   August 29, 1988

Sister Russell [a tour guide on Temple Square] seemed to be a particularly sensitive person who took a particular interest in me. Our discussion was interrupted when the next tour began. Shortly into that tour, she caught up to me and handed me a copy of the Book of Mormon, which contained your photograph and testimony and in which she had penned a most thoughtful message concerning what she termed "my mission." I read the book and prayed about my Temple Square experiences.

Upon my return home I discussed my experience with my family. My wife suggested I pursue it further, so I contacted the local bishop, who turned me over to the ward's missionaries.

My wife and I proceeded slowly, receiving the series of investigator lessons over a six-week period. In the meantime, my twenty-one-year-old son, who said he noticed a change in me, also contacted the missionaries, and he covered the investigator lessons in two weeks. He was baptized and confirmed on last July 27 and received the Aaronic Priesthood shortly thereafter.

Then on last August 31, I had the rare privilege of being baptized by my son. While still wet, I was confirmed and received the Aaronic Priesthood. Then I had my second rare privilege of the day and proceeded to baptize my wife.

The part you played in this revolutionary change in our relationship to God and in the change in our life-styles (my wife and I have broken a thirty-plus-year smoking habit) is deeply appreciated. It is our hope and prayer that we will be together in the celestial kingdom.

George Stanton
Johnson City, Tennessee

Dear Sister Valaitis,   April 19, 1987

I sincerely hope you will receive this letter. I tried to contact you when I returned to N. Y., but was unsuccessful. (I'm living in Utah now and attending Med. School. I was accepted!) Although you probably don't remember who I am, I wanted to write and thank you for taking the time to talk to me that afternoon, a few weeks ago, and patiently explain those things that I did not understand.

I did have the chance to tour Temple Square, although it was delayed a few days because of an accident in which I sustained a broken nose and several broken ribs. However, I'm very grateful for the opportunity of visiting such an awesome place. While there, I was able to obtain a copy of the Book of Mormon, and have read it twice with the intent of continuing to read it until I remember all that I want to know.

In the past I have never felt the need to associate with any religious affiliation. I believed that the only thing any religion could accomplish is to increase the amount of stress that would come into the lives of those that believe, when they try to conform to a structured set of guidelines.

I feel the Mormon church is different. I find that the more information that I receive, the more I want to know. It's like Thanksgiving dinner after a two-week abstinence from food.

All my life I have never been able to describe how I would feel at times, but when I read Second Nephi, chapter 27, verse 3 ["It shall be unto them, even as unto a hungry man which dreameth, and behold he eateth but he awaketh and his soul is empty"], it helped me to understand. People around me would keep telling me that I have everything for a happy and successful life, but I felt there was something more, not knowing I was leaving out the most essential part, the complete knowledge of God. . . .

Anne Bradford
Salt Lake City, Utah

Dear Mr. and Mrs. Andrus, July 14, 1987

Two missionary sisters called at my house one cold wet June evening, and asked to come in a while. We talked, and after about an hour they left, leaving the Book of Mormon, donated by yourselves. They asked if I would read three passages from it, and to ask God if the book were true. They would return the following week to discuss further. I reluctantly agreed.

After they left I read the marked passages, but was so intrigued that I also read several chapters that night. The remainder of the week I was unable to put the Book of Mormon aside. I would snatch any spare few moments in the day or evening to read from it. I knew it was true.

To summarize, after a few weeks of being taught by the missionaries, I was baptized into God's church on July 5, 1987.

Words cannot express the joy and happiness that your kind donation of the Book of Mormon has brought me and my children. I hope in any way that I also will be able to spread the word of God, and others will share in our joy to love and serve him. May God bless you.

Helen, Clair, Peter, Carolyn & Richard Hemmens
Luton, Bedfordshire, England

Dear Roman and Irva Andrus, June 17, 1987

You don't know me. I am Yasmin Stokes. I am thirteen years old and go to Ickfield High School. I have received your Book of Mormon from the missionaries. Sister Preacher from Walton Beach, Florida, USA, and Sister Bond from Fort Macleod, Alberta, Canada, who we have made friends with. My mum, stepdad, and brother are all studying our Book of Mormon and go to the church and my mum and I are hoping soon to be baptized. I am so pleased to have received your book and many thanks for your great photo of yourselves. I will write again if it's o.k. with you both and send snaps of all our family.

You would love my young brother Adam. He is five years old and has his own children's picture Book of Mormon and enjoys going to church and his class. Thanking you again for my book I will study each day and will let you know when I am to be baptized.

> "God Bless" from Yasmin Stokes and my family.
> Luton, Bedfordshire, England

Dear Brother England,   December 16, 1989

I have a missionary who is always in my mind as relating to the Book of Mormon placement program. His name is Sabar Yarkasih. In the year of 1982 as he went to a bookstore, he saw two ladies discussing, almost arguing, the Book of Mormon. He was interested in their discussion. They discussed its fallacy. As those two women left the stand, he went and picked up the book. He determined to buy it because he wanted to know the contents. The price was Rp 3.500, which was five times more expensive than buying it from the Church. As soon as he went home he read it; however, to his surprise he could not find any of its fallacy. Because of it, then, he went looking for the church.

For two years he worked across from the church building. He watched the church. He felt very much impressed about it, and very often he sat under the LDS Church sign in front of the building, yet he kept looking for a "Mormon" church. Finally in 1986, two sister missionaries went to where he was working to print their name cards. He got acquainted with them, and after receiving discussions for several months then he was baptized.

And in 1987, he went on his mission. The Book of Mormon placement was badly manipulated by some book salesmen. They sell it for prices several times higher than it costs. However, again, it is an evidence that nothing is impossible in the Lord. He can change a tragedy to a joyful ending and even blessings that can bless many souls.

President Effian Kadarusman
Indonesia Jakarta Mission

HE HEARD THE ZULU CHILDREN SINGING ALL OVER THE HILLS

DAVID AND VELA HAWKINS
Durban, South Africa

In March 1988 we were transferred to Durban, the second largest city in South Africa. We were assigned to work in the Kwa Mashu Branch of the Durban stake.

Kwa Mashu is a Zulu branch right on the edge of the great Kwa Zulu nation. This nation, geographically a part of South Africa, has a population of seven and a half million people. The first time we attended sacrament meeting in Kwa Mashu there were seventy-five Zulus present. We found no word to describe our feelings as we made that comparison of one to one hundred thousand.

The branch president is a fine young convert about twenty-eight years old. His mother-in-law is a Zulu witch doctor. He and his wife had three children before they went to the temple in Johannesburg to be sealed. Their little son born since then is the first Zulu born under the covenant.

The branch met in a lovely Ican building with a beautiful yard. Sister Hawkins attended Relief Society that first Sunday, but as she heard the Primary children singing "I Am a Child of God," she knew she would be in Primary from then on. The next day the stake Primary president visited in our flat and asked Sister Hawkins to work with the Primary in Kwa Mashu.

We were asked by the branch president to teach his eight-year-old daughter to prepare her for baptism. We began teaching on Tuesday and Thursday after school. Four little girls attended the first class. We played a tape of children singing "Jesus Came to John the Baptist" and taught that story. At the end of class we gave each girl one of our Articles of Faith cards and told them if they learned one by next class they would get a prize. One girl learned the first one and we gave her a little package of cookies (they call them biscuits, as the British do), and we were in business.

The class began to grow. We were teaching faith, repentance, etc. The children knew of Joseph Smith and the gold plates. One day we asked them to name a person in the Book of Mormon. They guessed Moses, Adam, and Abraham, but not a Book of Mormon character. What a great door was opened to us that day—what an exciting opportunity!

We began with First Nephi and moved on through the book. We not only told the stories but also taught the gospel principles. We borrowed filmstrips and pictures from wards in the Durban stake. We often stopped the filmstrips to point out and discuss the ship, Nephi, the Liahona, the gold plates, or angels not having wings, etc.

The children couldn't get enough of the Book of Mormon pictures. They liked to see them over and over and name the people therein. The all-time favorite was Abinadi before King Noah and the wicked priests. They wanted to know which priest was Alma. One of their favorite things was to role-play the stories. The Zulu children were little hams and loved to perform. They really made the characters come to life.

The heritage of the Zulu nation since the days of Shaka, their famous warrior king, has been fighting and killing. After we saw how enthusiastically the children role-played "Nephi Kills Laban" and "Ammon Cuts Off the Arms of His Enemies," we began really down-playing violence and stressing prayer and good works. Alma again came to our rescue. "The word" is mightier than the sword.

After each class we went home excited and happy about the special spirit that we felt among the children. One thing we loved was seeing how they would apply the teachings to their own lives. For example, when we were reviewing we asked what King Benjamin taught his people. Their answers were "Don't let your children quarrel and fight" and "When you help other people you are helping God." Then a little girl gave this answer: "If you have some cabbage, and your neighbor doesn't have any, give him some, even if he didn't work to raise some."

One day after we had taught the Ten Commandments from Mosiah 13 we asked the children to name some of the commandments. The first answer was always "Don't smoke." We just let that pass as a fine commandment. They named "Don't kill," "Don't steal," and so on. Then a little boy gave a version of "Thou shalt not covet": "Don't wish you had your neighbor's mule." When the Zulu children would tell the story or see the filmstrip of Joseph Smith going into the woods to pray, they would say, "So Joseph went out into the *bush* to pray."

When we got into Alma in the Book of Mormon we gave the greatest lesson of all on the Atonement. We taught of temporal and physical death. Those Zulu children loved hearing of the two great gifts our Savior gave to each of us — resurrection and forgiveness — if we will repent. From then on *repent* was a big word in their vocabularies. Whenever we asked what any prophet had taught, their first answer was "Repent." We showed *Man's Search for Happiness,* stopping often to point out how Grandpa lived and died, how his body was buried, and how his spirit went to Paradise. Then we had to tell of spirit prison, and eventually we presented the whole plan of salvation from pre-earth life to the three degrees of glory. It was a joy to see their eyes light up as they put the parts together and understood.

We could have baptized dozens of those children. In fact, many of them asked us to baptize them. Some asked Sister Hawkins if she would baptize them. (Another great teaching moment.) We had been instructed by our mission, stake, and branch presidents not to baptize children unless they had family members active in the Church. We would tell them to bring their parents for us to teach. This way we got some good converts. Elder Hawkins never did the baptizing or confirming but gave the Zulu priests and young elders the opportunity to perform those priesthood ordinances.

The best thing about our classes and Sunday Primary was the singing. The Zulus sang beautifully! The children heard a song a few times and then began to harmonize. We had heard children in many Primaries singing "Book of Mormon Stories" but never to compare with those children in Kwa Mashu singing and doing the actions. A song that so much touched our hearts was "Oh, How Lovely Was the Morning" sung by the children in Zulu. How blessed we were that the Primary's sacrament meeting program for 1988 included four new verses of "Book of Mormon Stories"! The children just loved to hear about Alma, Ammon, the two thousand sons of Helaman, and Samuel the Lamanite—to hear and then to sing. "The Golden Plates" was a new song to them and soon became a favorite. We taught "To Nephi, Seer of Olden Time." The children quickly learned that the iron rod is the word of God and that the word of God is found in the Book of Mormon and the Holy Bible. We also taught "We Are of the Army of Helaman," and when we asked who is our Captain Helaman, their quick reply was, President Ezra Taft Benson. We then asked them what we are fighting against. Their answer was, wicked and bad things.

When the class numbered in the sixties, we gave up the biscuits and Articles of Faith. After a long class we were just too tired to listen to Articles of Faith for an hour and a half—many children had learned all thirteen Articles of Faith and lots of scriptures. At our last class we had eighty-seven children present. Many of them were from the mean, rough sections of Kwa Mashu, but we had no problems with them. Elder Hawkins chose their leaders to play the tapes and projector. They became our leaders. We were not allowed to go to the Zulu homes, into their townships, or even to the chapel at night.

Our grand finale was the children presenting the remodeled version of the Primary sacrament meeting program.

Twenty-three Zulu children gave their stories and parts in Zulu, and a multitude of other children joined them in singing their songs in English. No prompting was necessary. They were proudly presenting their Book of Mormon program and they were prepared. It was the largest congregation ever at Kwa Mashu branch. The parents and older Zulus were most proud. The children had never performed for them before, and here they were teaching them the truths of the Book of Mormon. They all thanked and complimented us, but we just said, "Your children."

One man told us we had done a wonderful work. He told us he heard children saying Articles of Faith and singing Book of Mormon songs all over the hills of Kwa Mashu.

In the beginning the children spoke very little English, so all classes were taught with interpreters. At the end of the eight months, they had learned a lot of English and we had learned a bit of Zulu.

It was hard to leave South Africa, and especially Kwa Mashu. The last Sunday, as we said our farewells, one dear Zulu sister thanked us, as she had done many times before, for teaching her children the Book of Mormon. She started to cry and said, "Water has been coming out of my face all day, because you are going away." Water came out of our faces, too.

He Felt He Had Cheated the Lord Out of Forty Years

Perris Jensen
Cardiff, Wales

Harold Say was an employee of *The Echo*, the most widely circulated newspaper published in Wales. He had been exposed to the gospel for years but had never cared enough about it to really investigate. My wife, Gwen, and I began calling upon him in 1966 at the request of the young missionaries, who had pretty well given up hope of interesting him. Because we were older he paid more attention to us, and we finally got him started reading the Book of Mormon. He got about halfway through when, one evening, he declared to us, "The book is divine. No mere mortal could have produced it. If it is divine, then the man who brought it forth must have been a prophet; and if he was a prophet, then the church which he established must have been God's church. It is all done up in one package." A few days later I baptized him, and at last report he was still a faithful member.

William Bailey was an associate of Harold Say. He also lived in Barry, a village not far from Cardiff, Wales, and he also worked for *The Echo*. Where Brother Say was passive, Brother Bailey was antagonistic, mean. His wife once remarked to us, out of his presence, "You'll never get anywhere with him. He is the most intolerant man in the world." Each night we called on him we battled. We really went round and round. But each night, as we left, he would remark, "You'll be back, won't you." We assured him we would be back just as long as he would tolerate us. During the week he spent his spare time in the Cardiff public library reading anti-Mormon books to try to find something that he could use to tie us up. He had tied the young missionaries up in knots by digging up old accounts of anti-Mormon stuff that they had never heard about. I was a new challenge, and he was determined to beat me down as he had done with the younger missionaries. Week after week we battled. Then one night, in the middle of a question, he stopped with the remark, "No! That's wrong. I'm through asking questions. Now you teach me." Then we began to get somewhere.

After much effort we induced him to begin reading the Book of Mormon. A few weeks later, when we were discussing the Atonement, he remarked that the only reason for Christ's mission was to teach us by example how we should live. We had discussed the Atonement many times, but apparently our teaching had gone right over his head. By this time we were on a friendly basis, so that I could kid with him a bit. In fact we had talked about the Book of Mormon, and he had asked me if I had ever noticed the great difference in literary style between Nephi and his brother Jacob.

When he spoke of literary style I asked him what he had observed. He explained, "Nephi writes with great difficulty. He has a hard time explaining himself. It's like driving an automobile with the brakes on. But oh, when you come to Jacob, he's a writer after my own heart. He just sails through the waves in a yacht."

When Brother Bailey remarked that the Savior's sole mission was to teach us by example how we should live, I challenged him, "Who taught you how to read? I don't think you can read very well, can you?" It was a dangerous remark, but it got his attention. Imagine asking a newspaperman if he can read well. He bristled up with his old antagonism, "What do you mean?" I said, "Let's go back and read a couple of chapters and see what you have been reading about the Atonement."

We read aloud chapters 2 and 9 of Second Nephi. He was humbled and apologized for his antagonism, "I see what you mean. I was reading only for the literary aspect. I think I better start again at the beginning."

The second time around he read for the doctrine. He got over into Alma, where Alma was baptizing in the Waters of Mormon, and he was ready for baptism. Even more, he was concerned about his dead grandson, who had never been baptized. We had already explained about baptism for the dead, but again it appeared to have gone over his head. We reminded him that he himself had never been baptized. He responded that he had been thinking about that, too, and thought perhaps on his birthday he would be baptized. My wife spoke up, "Why wait until then? You might be dead by then, or we could be, or we might be transferred." Three days later I baptized him. Within six weeks he was branch president. His zeal against had now become zeal for the work.

I had no part in the conversion of Brother Bateman, of Woodsetten, near Birmingham, but I heard him bear his testimony in church. His wife was a member, which was fine with him, because whenever she went to church he could go to the pub. One evening she was going to MIA. He lay down to relax a bit until she was gone, so he could go to the pub, but he fell fast asleep. When he awoke it was too late to go to the pub, but right beside him was the Book of Mormon. With nothing else to do he began to read. It interested him and he continued to read, but he was not about to let his wife know that he was reading it, so he hid the book except when she was away. She was amazed when he announced, one day, that he was ready to be baptized, even without the missionaries having taught him. Or did she secretly know what he was doing, but felt it best to keep quiet about it?

The place the Book of Mormon played in the story of Captain Jones is somewhat different. Captain Jones, a former sea captain, was blind. He was sitting on a park bench one day when a young lady approached from one side, reading a book as she walked. At the same time a man, whose name the captain never learned, was approaching from the other side. When the two came together, right in front of where the captain was sitting, the man asked the young lady what she was reading. She replied that she was reading the Book of Mormon. Then he passed on and was gone. Now you don't accost people on the street and ask them what they are reading, but it did happen this time.

Captain Jones heard what the lady said and called to her. He told her he wanted to know more about that Book of Mormon. She turned out to be a local missionary, and she was most anxious to meet with him, with her companion, and tell him about the Book of Mormon. But she was curious to know where he had ever heard about the Book of Mormon. He explained that forty years earlier, when he was a young sailor, he had left his ship in San Pedro, California, and was making his way across the States to the east coast. He entered Utah at St. George and, being out of money, stopped to work for a time. He painted houses. He was in Utah for a whole year before he finally went on into Wyoming. He heard a great deal about the Church and the gospel. He said, "The Lord called me to become a member, but I didn't." From that point on he had not heard the word *Mormon* until the young lady responded to the question of the "amiable stranger," as the captain called the man who was passing.

The lady missionaries worked with the captain for several weeks, but could get nowhere with him, as far as baptism was concerned. Finally they asked my wife and me to call on him. He was friendly enough and willing to listen to us, but he kept insisting he was not ready for baptism because he was not worthy. It was quite awhile before we determined why he was reluctant. He finally admitted that the reason he felt unworthy was because he had been, as he called it, "called by the Lord forty years earlier," and he had thus "cheated the Lord out of forty years' service." This gave me the clue to his resistance, and I reminded him of the story of the prodigal son. I asked him point-blank if it was better for the son to return to his father or remain with the pigs. He responded, "I get the point. I guess I should be baptized." But he explained that he had emphysema and had to go to the hospital the very next day.

We visited him several times in the hospital, where he spent his time preaching to the nurses. They told us he pestered them to death with his urging them to read the Book of Mormon. Then one day we went to the hospital and he was gone. The nurses were very much upset. They said he just got up and left without saying anything to anybody. We scooted over to his apartment and found him there. We asked him why, when they had not yet finished their course of treatments. He said he didn't know why. I told him, "I know why you left. You left so you could be baptized." He said he was ready, if the doctor would permit it. We phoned the doctor, and he said it was okay if he were baptized in a heated pool. I arranged with the missionaries to have the pool ready a couple of days later.

When we arrived for the baptism, the chapel and the pool were stone cold. The heating plant had failed; but the captain said go ahead anyway, and I baptized him. The captain then returned to the hospital for the rest of the treatment. Just at that time we were transferred from Cardiff up into Birmingham. We didn't see the captain again until about a year later when we came back on a short visit. A new chapel was being constructed in Cardiff. The brick masons were doing a sloppy job, and the supervisor had required them to tear down and relay some of the brickwork. We found Captain Jones at the chapel site as a volunteer worker, cleaning off the old mortar from the torn down bricks, so that they could be re-laid. He was healthy, cheerful, and happy in spite of his blindness. Still staunch in the faith.

IT CAME WITH HER TESTIMONY IN IT

JOHN P. DANIEL
Littleton, Colorado

Even though I did not receive a Book of Mormon until I was sixteen, the first time I became acquainted with any of the unique doctrines put forth by the Book of Mormon was when I was thirteen years old. My social studies class was studying the conquest of Mexico by Cortez. The teacher explained that a handful of conquistadors were able to conquer the mighty Aztec nation, not because of superior power but because the Aztecs mistook Cortez for a bearded white man who had visited them centuries before and who had promised to return one day. That day, as I walked home from my bus stop, I pondered this, and the conclusion was given to me that the bearded white man for whom the Aztecs waited was none other than Jesus Christ. When this thought settled upon my mind, I felt assured that it was true. It was, in fact, a conclusion that struck me with such force that it was easily recalled at later times.

I have always been proud of my American Indian descent, even though it is very slight. Therefore, stories, documentaries, and anything else dealing with the Indians have been very

interesting to me. It was because of this interest that I read a
book by Anna Lee Waldo called *Sacajawea* (Avon Books, 1978),
a novel about the Indian woman who led Lewis and Clark on
their expedition. The book spoke of a tribe of Indians that
performed a ceremony in which boys became men. This ceremony was performed by placing skewers through the muscles
of the chest or of the back, tieing ropes to the skewers, and
raising the boy off the ground until his body weight caused
the skewers to tear through the muscles. This was done in
similitude of another man who had been lifted up a long time
before. As I read this, I felt that it was another piece of evidence
that my conclusion was true, that Jesus Christ *did* visit America.

I cannot remember whether I read *Sacajawea* before or
after I received the Book of Mormon, and I don't really think
it matters. I didn't read the Book of Mormon when I first
received it. Perhaps that was because the contents weren't really
explained to me. I received it from a very close friend named
Mara, whom I had been dating for several months. I knew she
was a Mormon, but we seldom discussed the Church. When
we did discuss it, we spoke of its organizational structure or
spoke of the gospel in general terms — things I already knew
and believed. A peaceful feeling blanketed me when we talked.
These discussions seem to have been the catalyst for her giving
me a Book of Mormon. When I opened it, I was furious — and
I didn't know why (a common reaction to the book). But I
kept the book for two reasons: (1) it came from one of my
best friends — one of the few people in the world who showed
love for me and (2) it came with her testimony written in it.

When I first received the Book of Mormon, I read Mara's
testimony and was moved that she gave it to me because she
wanted me to have an opportunity for eternal life. Then I read
the testimony of the Prophet Joseph Smith as it is published
at the beginning of the Book of Mormon. I say, "I read it," but
"watched it" would be more accurate, for the images in my
mind were clear and precise. How I wish I had understood,
then, that the book is the scripture from the ancient Indians.

But I did not — and the images from my reading did not compel me to continue to read. Therefore, the Book of Mormon went on a shelf.

Later, Mara and I stopped seeing each other, completed high school, and went to college. She went to BYU while I went first to Colorado State and then to Texas Tech. The Book of Mormon tagged along in these travels but was never touched. While I was at Texas Tech, however, events did occur that eventually led me to read the Book of Mormon.

The first event was an experience that is so sacred to me that I will only mention that I learned that Jesus Christ is the King of Kings. I was also commanded to find the truth — the word of God — with a promise I would know it when I found it. From this experience I gained the incentive and desire to find out all I could about God and what He wanted me to do.

During my search, I again found myself perusing statements about ancient American beliefs. My English class required me to write a research paper, so I obtained permission from the teacher to write a comparison/contrast paper on mythologies of the world. While reading about those of South America, I found a myth that spoke of a virgin who had conceived miraculously and brought forth a mighty leader. I was impressed with how closely the myth resembled some aspects of the story of Mary, the mother of Jesus Christ. I treasured this up in my heart.

My time at Texas Tech was also a time of learning to listen to and to understand God. Dreams that taught me and inspired me became frequent. One of the more common elements in the dreams was spending time with Mara. In 1984 I began to feel an intense desire to see her again. Fortunately summer break soon arrived and I had my opportunity. While we dated, I felt my old feelings return, and I strongly desired to ask Mara to be my wife (a situation that would never be). She refused my proposal because I could not take her to the temple. She wanted me to join the Church but not because of her — and I couldn't join it for any other reason than that I believed joining it was the correct thing to do. This experience of a rejected marriage proposal gave me the desire to find out if the Mormon church was true.

When I went home that night I pondered the events of the day and suddenly remembered that Mara had given me a Book of Mormon. I determined to read it, but first I had to find it. I vaguely recalled seeing it when I had packed to come home, so it was most likely buried under a pile of books that were still in boxes. Much to my surprise, I found it in the first box I looked in, face up, and under only one other book. Shrugging off this coincidence, I commenced to read. As I progressed through the Book of Mormon, I learned of the origins of a group of ancient Americans. I grew to love them. I mourned when they suffered and exulted when they were righteous. I learned how God deals with His children. And as I read I hungered to learn more. I was compelled to read on.

I met friends. Alma taught me how to experiment with the word and be born again. Ammon showed me how to serve. I wept—rather, sobbed—with joy as Ammon praised his God while reflecting on the joy of his labors. Then, after I had watched a people waver between righteousness and wickedness, I received a confirmation of the truth I had learned as a thirteen-year-old. I heard my King, the Lord Jesus Christ, speak to my new friends, telling them that they were his other sheep and members of the house of Israel. Jesus Christ *did* visit America.

Through this whole experience, three emotions filled my heart. First, I felt a love I had been seeking since my childhood, a love I had lost from some time before I could remember but which I had felt briefly from time to time. Second, I felt a peace that filled me and caused all problems and difficulties to melt into insignificance. Third, I felt a joy beyond anything I ever dreamed possible, yet which did not compare to what would come later.

I began to get hints in my teens of truths I would later know. These hints came from temporal and spiritual sources. Now I have the knowledge that can come only from purely spiritual sources. I am grateful for faithful members of the Church and committed missionaries who helped me to understand the meaning of the beautiful feelings I had while reading the Book of Mormon.

WE FELT AN INTENSE AND INDEFINABLE EXCITEMENT

NOEL OWEN
Anglesey, Wales

It started in the fall of 1964 when we first met Lamond and Marta Tullis—the first Latter-day Saints we had ever met. Pat and I, together with our baby daughter Sian, had travelled from our home in Wales to the east coast of the USA, where I was to take up a research fellowship in the chemistry department at Harvard University. We had rented an apartment on the outskirts of Boston and, on our return from a six-week-long journey by car wherein we had travelled the country from the east coast to the west coast and back again, we were very interested to find that a new family had moved into a neighboring apartment. The car license plates of our new neighbors told us that they were from Utah, and we were anxious to meet them and hopeful that they might prove friendly.

It was not until the following day that I had an opportunity to meet the newcomers. Upon exchanging a few introductory words with Lamond, I learnt that they were "Mormons." I remember exclaiming that that was interesting and that they would have to tell us more about themselves, since the only thing that I knew about Mormons was that they were, or had been, polygamous—and this was largely gleaned from the Western tales of Zane Grey! On my return from work the following evening, I learnt that Pat had met and talked with Marta. The initial conversation had proceeded along those so-familiar lines: "Would you like to come over for a cup of tea?"

Marta replied with a smile, "I'm afraid that I don't drink tea."

"Oh, then come for a cup of coffee!"

"I'm afraid that I don't drink coffee either, but I'd love to come over and visit with you anyway."

We have laughed many times together as we recalled that first meeting. But it was the beginning of a great and lasting friendship with Lamond and Marta Tullis. We spent many hours together as two young families would, and we plied them with questions about what was to us this fascinating new religion. I well remember how we followed the logical development of Lamond's argument so far, only to find a gap that their faith could bridge but over which our skepticism could not venture. For example, we found it difficult to accept that Joseph Smith had seen our Heavenly Father and His Son Jesus Christ and had been taught by the angel Moroni. It is also probably true that at this time we did not feel the need of changing our religious beliefs. I cannot remember any pressure coming from them, only an occasional outburst of frustration from Marta, "If only you could see things as we see them!"

At the same time, however, we recognized that there was something very special about the Tullis family, something that we had not experienced before. We were particularly impressed with the way Lamond and Marta were bringing up their two boys — the strong family love and respect was obvious, but kindly discipline also played a part, and the whole family relationship was one that we realized was excellent. We were quite amazed that Michael (a three-year-old) could pray aloud quite unselfconsciously with his family.

During our year together, Lamond and Marta gave us two books. One was a copy of the Book of Mormon and the other was a pictorial book called *Meet the Mormons*. We enjoyed looking at the pictures, but sadly the Book of Mormon remained on our bookshelves largely unread for the next eight years. After returning to North Wales, we would see the missionaries from time to time, but though we always made them welcome in our home, we were convinced that they could not tell us anything about the Church and the Book of Mormon that we did not already know.

In 1972, while I was working for six months at the University of British Columbia, we travelled to Utah to see the Tullis family again, and we visited Temple Square, where we were impressed in a spiritual way by the Visitors' Center and all that we saw. On our return to Britain, we were once again contacted by the missionaries and once more found ourselves falling into the same pattern of extending hospitality and conversation without commitment on our part.

Then two things changed. The first was that the Lord sent to our area of Wales one of the best prepared and most tenacious missionaries that he could possibly have chosen, and the second was that Pat and I began to realize that our four children were growing up without the religious foundation of regular church attendance. Pat and I had been unable to agree on the question of which church we should frequent, although we were both agreed that church attendance should be a family affair. Consequently our contact with formal religious groups was somewhat sporadic. After being visited by Elder Mickelson and his companions for several months and after continuously frustrating their attempts to complete a single discussion by constantly asking innumerable questions, we eventually decided that we would start listening to the elders' discussions without interruption and that when the discussions were completed we would make our decision.

In hindsight, I now realize that this is how the Holy Ghost works. This young missionary humbled us sufficiently to have us kneel down in our living room as a family and pray together. At the same time, he pleaded with us to commit ourselves to read parts of the Book of Mormon. I remember very clearly that after reading from the Book of Mormon one day, I turned to Pat and said, "You know, the more I read this book, the more I'm beginning to think that it's true!" It was not long before we both felt this same remarkable feeling; at last we had grasped it! With this remarkable change in our attitude, it seemed no longer difficult to believe in Joseph Smith's first vision and in the translation of the gold plates. The social implications of accepting the restored gospel of Jesus Christ were still to be a slight problem, especially to Pat, who loved her "cup of tea," but even these soon lost their apparent importance in the light of this exciting new truth that we had "discovered."

I was baptized in an ancient-looking font at a house that had been converted into a meetingplace about forty miles from our home, and two weeks later, after receiving the Aaronic Priesthood, I baptized Pat and our two oldest children. At that time, the Church in our area of North Wales consisted of a very small and scattered congregation of members, most of whom, however, had very strong testimonies of the gospel. In the early days and weeks following our baptism, we felt an intense and indefinable excitement, and I clearly recall driving to work one morning, glancing at the people I passed and thinking that they must be able to tell that I was now LDS, merely from looking at me. As well as the joy that we felt, this period was not without its challenges, and it was our testimony of the truthfulness of the Book of Mormon that often kept us going.

As I Lay There, Holding the Book in My Hands, I Knew

Mark P. Rasmussen
Bountiful, Utah

I had always considered myself as basically a good person, a strong believer in God and Jesus Christ and His teachings. I was a believer in the Holy Bible, and having grown up in Bountiful, Utah, and having a wife and children of the LDS faith, I had a high regard for the LDS Church and its members.

I lived in the Bountiful 40th Ward, where I had developed many friendships with its members.

Anyway, I suddenly began to realize that I had done very little in my adult life to improve myself as a person (spiritually), and I felt that "okay" was no longer good enough. I wanted to, and did, begin to be more supportive and involved with my family's Church activities. Reflecting back now, I remember something that my father had said to me one evening during our deer hunt in the late fall of 1986. I don't recall how the subject came up, but Dad said that not only should I support my family in the Church but I should go and participate and be with them. He indicated that I was not being a good example. This message stayed with me and, I am sure now, had a great deal to do with my desire to improve myself, even though I didn't realize it at the time.

During the last few months of 1987, I gradually became more active in Church activities with my family. Then one day my wife, Lynne, asked me if I would attend our ward family night at the Visitors' Center at Temple Square with her and the children. I said yes and felt quite good about it at the time, seeing it as an opportunity to spend some time with my family doing something that I knew meant a lot to them. However, as the day drew near for this event, I became more and more tentative about it until by that evening, when time to go approached, I was totally irritated that I had ever agreed to go— so irritated, in fact, that I found something to argue with my wife about. I had such a bad attitude and disposition that she finally left without me. But then, she tells me now, she realized that it was very important that I should go with them, so important that she felt that it was Satan trying to keep me from going. She turned around and came home, hoping that I would still go with them. She was not about to allow Satan to have his way.

As soon as my wife left without me, I felt terrible, knowing that how I had been acting was wrong and not knowing why I had even acted that way. I wasn't sure what to do and was feeling pretty low, so I was really glad but very humble when she returned and asked me again if I would still go with them. I agreed, and we left together. When we arrived at the Visitors' Center, I felt better, but I was really still not very interested in what we were going to do. I think I was getting a little irritated again, wondering why I had agreed to do this. But as I began to see familiar faces, my attitude softened. Then we began to look around the center because we were a little early for the meeting to begin. I wandered up the spiral ramp and at the top suddenly I was standing before a huge statue of Jesus Christ, the *Christus*. Words alone cannot describe the feeling that overwhelmed me as I looked up at my Savior's image, but it was almost as if He was there, and His spirit truly was.

I felt shame and sorrow for the things that I had done wrong and for the wrongs that had been done to Him, and yet I felt enlightened, full of hope and joy for the future. Finally, with tear-filled eyes, I turned and walked back down the ramp, avoiding others as I collected my emotions.

I was very attentive for the remainder of the evening. Later, I found out by a sign or some literature that was passed out, that one could obtain a free copy of the Book of Mormon as he or she left the Center. I knew immediately that I wanted to do that and kept it in my mind until just before we were ready to leave. I told my wife, and I went to get *my* copy of the Book of Mormon. Even though I now had a desire to read the Book of Mormon, I don't know why I felt I needed my own copy. There are many copies in my home and had been for the almost seventeen years Lynne and I had been married. I had never had a desire to read the Book of Mormon before, but now I did, and I desired to have my own copy.

As we drove home, I reflected on the presentations and exhibits we had seen at the Visitors' Center. As we discussed them as a family, I am sure my family could sense my change of attitude. But I did not tell them how excited I really was or how anxious I was to get home and begin to read my Book of Mormon. I was afraid of building up their hopes and did not want to feel pressured, so I didn't say much about my feelings for a long time, even after I had been reading the Book of Mormon for a couple of months.

As I prepared for bed that evening, I lay down in my bed, propped my head up on my pillows and prepared to begin reading my Book of Mormon. As I lay there holding the book in my hands, I knew, even before I opened it, that it was true. I was about to discover the truth. I also had a very strange feeling, which affected me very deeply, that I had always known that the Book of Mormon was true. I had silently prayed to my Father in Heaven to let me know the truth of what I was about to read, and my prayer was answered before I began. I believe now that one reason I did resist reading the Book of Mormon, as others have and will, is that we all know that its teachings are true, and if we read them, we will be obligated to abide by them.

In the months that followed, I pursued my study of the Book of Mormon, reading as often and for as long as possible, always not wanting to put it down. I also had the opportunity to attend with my wife weekly study classes on some of the basic beliefs of the Church at the home of Bishop David Lewis.

After frequent visits by my home teacher, David Hansen, my interest began to grow. Then Brother Newell Bryson, one of the stake missionaries, asked if I would be interested in having the regular full-time missionaries come with him to teach me. After the third lesson, the missionaries asked me if I would be willing to be baptized and set a date for it. I knew that I had to make a final commitment to myself and to Jesus Christ in order to continue to improve in my life and progress spiritually. I made that commitment and was baptized on August 27, 1988.

I continue to study the Book of Mormon, reading it through now for the second time. As I become accustomed to being a member of the Church and as I struggle to progress as a spirit and a person, my enthusiasm for my responsibilities as a member may waver a bit, but my knowledge of the truth, of the

Book of Mormon, the gospel of Jesus Christ, will always be immovable. And I know that if I will read and study and ponder its teachings and pray, I will continue to progress toward my goal of returning to my Father in heaven.

Cousin Elsie Put the Book into My Hands

Dorothy E. Watkins Watkins
Nottingham, England

I was born in Nottingham, England, of goodly parents: James Willie (Will) Watkins and Eva Charlotte Dexter Watkins, on January 18, 1911— their second child. I have truly loved the Lord since I was a little child, and I acknowledge His hand upon me throughout my life. I was brought up in the Church of Christ, going to Sherwood Street Chapel every Sunday with my parents and brothers, with Sunday School in the afternoon. I always loved to be there.

When I was fifteen, a Welsh evangelist preached at our chapel, which greatly moved me, inviting us to give our hearts to the Lord and come unto Him. At the end they played "Just as I am, without one plea—but that Thy blood was shed for me—O Lamb of God I come!" I was fighting to hold the tears back but could not, and I sprang out of my seat and ran down the aisle to the front, tears streaming down my face. Then I turned and saw that my cousin and dearest lifelong friend, Joyce Rest, and her brother Philip, two years younger, had followed me. I was so glad; and the congregation shouted, "Hallelujah! Praise the Lord!" Two days later, we were all baptized by my uncle Percy White, husband to Mother's sister, Grace Dexter.

The first persons in the Dexter family to join the Lord's church, The Church of Jesus Christ of Latter-day Saints, were my grandfather Dexter's sister Annie Dexter Noble and her daughter Julia Troward Noble, who were taught by two American missionaries. Later, Annie's husband, Abraham Noble, was baptized and also their other daughters, Dora, Hilda and Betty (twins), and Elsie Marian, the youngest.

They all emigrated to Utah in 1912. Great-aunt Annie and Uncle Abe visited England when I was a child to try to convert their relatives. They came to our home, and their visit was the first time I heard of Mormonism. Because of polygamy, my mother was bitterly opposed to it. My dear father was a very religious and kind man and loved the Holy Bible, and they had long discussions, but there were no conversions except one, Annie's sister Elizabeth Dexter (Aunt Lizzie), who emigrated to Utah and married an American.

The years passed, and then came World War II. At the outbreak of war on October 9, 1939, I gave up my job to join the Civil Defense as an ambulance driver and in 1941 became a convoy driver in the Women's Military Services. I was demobilized in December, 1945, and tried to pick up the threads of the life I had left in 1939. One never-to-be-forgotten day, dear Cousin Elsie Marian Noble McCune, Great-aunt Annie's daughter and my mother's first cousin, came to visit us at the end of her mission in Wales. We had a nice meal and visit together, and I felt her loving spirit. Before she left, Cousin Elsie put a Book of Mormon into my hands and said, "Dorothy, if I leave you this Book of Mormon, will you read it?" And I replied, "Yes, I certainly will read it!"

I did read it — and *loved* it — and often said to Mother, who sat with me at the fireside, reading the deaths in the Nottingham *Evening Post,* "Oh! Do read this, Mother!" but she wouldn't and finally said she was not interested.

As I read the Book of Mormon, I knew that it was true, just as much as the Bible, and was another testament of the Lord Jesus Christ. Even so, I put to the test the promise found in Moroni 10:4–5. One night I knelt at my bedside and asked God, my Heavenly Father, in the name of Christ, to confirm to me that the Book of Mormon was true.

I fell asleep but later suddenly awakened and sat straight

up in bed, wide awake. Immediately, I felt an outpouring of the Holy Ghost upon me, enveloping my whole being, and felt filled with Light and Truth. It was wonderful! With joy I cried out, "Yes, it is *true!* The Book of Mormon is *true!*"

Later on, I was given the gospel discussions by two young missionaries from Utah. I drank my last cup of tea and my last cup of coffee, having learned the Word of Wisdom from the Lord, accepted the law of tithing, and was baptized into the Lord's church on a terribly foggy Saturday night at Nottingham Branch Chapel on January 14, 1961. Elder Hill baptized me, and I came up from the water full of joy and feeling cleansed. The chapel was a double bay-windowed house named Trentmore, on Musters Road, West Bridgeford, Nottingham. Its center wall had been removed, and the baptismal font was underneath the floorboards.

Derek and Muriel Cuthbert and their children were members, and what terrific leadership was theirs. Muriel could "move mountains"! About three weeks after I was baptized, dear Bishop Albert Green, now deceased, called me to be first counselor in the Relief Society presidency.

What a debt of gratitude I owe to dear Cousin Elsie Noble McCune, who placed the Book of Mormon in my hands, leading me into the Lord's church! Eternal blessings are mine. Both Elsie and Clarence have been instruments in the hands of the Lord in bringing to pass these blessings.

When I left the grey shores of England that snowy day, January 20, 1969, I knew not what the future held. I little knew that on March 1, 1972, I would be married in the Salt Lake Temple for time and all eternity to none other than United States Senator Arthur Vivian Watkins.

But I was! And it was the Lord who brought us together. This I know without a shadow of a doubt. It is a very precious and treasured story. I praise the Lord for all His loving guidance and care of me throughout my life.

I CAME TO UNDERSTAND CHRIST'S WORDS WHEN I JOINED HIS CHURCH
Danuta Mandziak
Warsaw, Poland

Though I was a nun, I lived without God and His love for twenty-eight years. I believed in God, but I didn't believe God. I never gave much thought to His holy gospel, to His teachings, in which He said, "I am the Way, the Truth, and the Life." These words of my Savior I came to understand at the moment I joined His holy church of the latter days.

On the 27th of July, 1986, in the afternoon hours, as I was walking along Nowy Swiat Street, I noticed a plaque informing me that here was a bureau of information of The Church of Jesus Christ of Latter-day Saints. After some hesitation I decided to walk in and ask what kind of church this was — what about "Mormons," whether one more heresy had sprung up in the doctrine of Jesus Christ, whether again, alongside nine hundred denominations, had arisen a new one. I went inside. That which I experienced inside this church I am setting down on paper so that those who come in contact with the Mormon church will know that it is really of Christ and that the believing Christians who constitute this church — this wonderful Mormon family — are children of God.

When I first came into contact with the church of Jesus Christ — actually with the missionaries, wonderful people dedicated to God, Brother Juliusz and Sister Dorothy Fussek — I was wonderfully satisfied. In a very simple, cheerful manner they taught me about the goodness of God and how He cares for me and wants me to do His holy will. That was rather shocking to me: How is it that God is love? I, a student of theology, am supposed to submit to God's love? That's impossible. I'm supposed to cross out all the dogmas of the pope, throw away the Catholic church, and join an "unknown" church? Impossible. At the end of our first meeting, the Fusseks gave me a Book of Mormon. When I arrived home (I lived, as I still do, in a boarding room), I placed the Book of Mormon on the table. The landlady with whom I lived, seeing that I had a book "of the devil," within five minutes ordered me to leave the house. And there, at that moment, occurred my tragedy. I was left without a roof over my head and without help of any kind. At this point the brothers and sisters of the Church of Jesus Christ (Mormons) helped me both spiritually and materially. One of the Mormon brethren found me a room at the residence of a certain artist. I lived there only one day, because this "great painter" threw me out after several hours.

So, again, a tragedy. I had nowhere to live, nothing to eat, and was without money. How can I live? Why am I visited with suffering, stumbling, and disappointment? And here, again, the Fusseks came to my aid. These two excellent people gave me a true Christian hand. They taught me that God was testing me and that he had an important errand for me. He wanted to ascertain whether I am strong and whether I trust in him.

These two very jolting incidents led me to study the Book of Mormon, for I had not yet been able to do so. I met often with Brother Juliusz and Sister Dorothy, who helped me to understand the Book of Mormon. I came regularly to the Sunday services of the Church. In a manner not evident or comprehensible to me, one of my acquaintances found me a place to live. Gradually my life began to come together.

In October I went on a vacation to my parents' place in the country. When I shared with them that I believed in the true God and in His holy scripture, the Book of Mormon, within fifteen minutes they told me to leave home. Again a blow— without parents, without a parental home, without the sense that I'm needed, or that anyone loves me—again an experience to test whether God exists.

Yes, He exists! I will choose Him and His wonderful doctrine and His pure, impartial love. He taught me that if I love parents more than I love Him, I am not worthy of Him. At this point the Fusseks came again to help me. They took the place of my physical parents and strengthened me spiritually and continued to bolster me. I love them very much. Every time I went to them, I felt that they loved me—every smile, gesture, word took the place of my parental home. The three instances of changing residences (twice being thrown out of my room and once from the home of my parents) strengthened my faith in God. I came to know that this is a test—my Father in Heaven is testing me, just as a smith tries his iron in the fire. My love for God began to increase, and I felt ever more strongly that I am His child.

Now, again came an important moment in my life—preparation for baptism. And here again with spiritual help came Brother Juliusz, my dear "Daddy," and Sister Dorothy, my most wonderful "Mom." With great love and devotion they prepared me, and November 21 at 6 P.M. was one of the most miraculous days of my life. In the presence of brothers, sisters, and investigators, I received the baptism of Jesus Christ. Brother Juliusz performed the baptism. There were tears and congratulations from those present. Today I tell everybody that I am very happy. I found God and partook of His love. I thank thee, Good Father in Heaven, for that miraculous moment—that You are in me and I, Father, in Thee.

I am writing this memoir for my spiritual parents, Brother Juliusz and Sister Dorothy, at their request, so that when they go back home, across the ocean, they will not forget that in Poland there is someone who loves them, who remembers them, and who is praying for them. (Translated by Walter Whipple.)

THE WOMAN IN SIBERIA ASKED, "ARE YOU A BELIEVER?"

BARBARA ALLEN KOVALENKO
Novosibirsk, USSR

On a recent trip to the Soviet Union, my husband, Gene, and

I spent a few days in the Siberian city of Novosibirsk. There we were warmly welcomed and entertained by a group of people who had organized as citizen diplomats interested in promoting friendship with our people.

As we walked down a frosty street one day, leaving a Russian Orthodox church service in a dazzling, recently restored church, one of the ladies of the group, who reminded me of many of my Relief Society sisters, began talking to me in English. As it turned out, she is a linguist specializing in northern Siberian languages and English at the technical institute there. She soon asked me, "Are you a believer?" When I got over my surprise and said yes, she replied, "It is natural to believe; yes, yes, it is natural."

We had brought an extra Book of Mormon to Siberia, and I thought at once that I might have found the person to give it to. As we became better acquainted over the next couple of days, that seemed more and more the right thing to do. So when we were in her home one evening I asked her if she would like to have a book we in our culture hold very dear.

She said at first, "But you must not give away something so precious!"

After I assured her that I could easily get another copy, she said she would very much like to have it. I inscribed it for her and asked her to begin by reading Moroni 10:4. She held it reverently and said, "This will be our family book; we will pass it from generation to generation."

The next day I saw her again. She told me, "I have been looking at the book you gave me, and I can tell it is a book to read many times." She asked if I would write to her regularly, so now I have a wonderful correspondent in that far-off, beautiful land, someone who, in addition to being a new friend, has promised to tell me what she thinks about this testament of Jesus Christ.

Dear Barbara: January 18, 1989

. . . I read your book regularly. Strange as it may seem, I

understand everything. But I don't keep all the events in my
mind, so I reread some pages and enjoy it. Thank you. For me
it's quite a new experience.

Galina Kurkin
Novosibirsk, USSR

CONVERSIONS

In this section are the personal witnesses of thirty-one converts
who have come to know the Book of Mormon is true scripture
and have been brought to Christ by it. The stories are from all
over the world, by people of immensely varied backgrounds
and conditions, but they reveal some interesting similarities
in the way the Book of Mormon affects people. Many are drawn
to it by what seems a physical power. Many feel a tangible
burning or "electric" sensation, sometimes directly as they
touch or hold it, sometimes all through their body as they read
it. The accounts cover nearly one hundred sixty years, but the
first and the last are remarkably similar, down to the details
of being unable to stop reading and of seeing visions of the
book's influence. Of course, most are brought to a direct spiritual
witness by accepting the invitation of Moroni to read the book
carefully and to ask God, with real intent, if it is true. The
answer comes in a variety of ways — a voice, an inner peace, a
sense of divine presence or actual beings, an undeniable and
permanent feeling of being changed, an ability to forgive someone who has injured them, an intellectual conviction of truth —
but with similar feelings of both joy and responsibility. Many
witnesses tell of the powerful effect upon them of the words
of Christ and the account of his visit to ancient America. Quite
a few are brought to tears and to a softening of their hearts
by the Spirit when they read of Christ's weeping in his yearning
love for the Nephite children.

EATING WAS A BURDEN, AND
I PREFERRED READING TO SLEEP

PARLEY P. PRATT
Palmyra, New York

The following account is from the Autobiography of Parley
Parker Pratt, *edited by Parley P. Pratt [son] (Salt Lake City:
Deseret Book, 1975), pages 36–40.)*

We visited an old Baptist deacon by the name of Hamlin.
After hearing of our appointment for evening, he began to tell
of a *book*, a STRANGE BOOK, a VERY STRANGE BOOK! in his
possession, which had been just published [1830]. This book,
he said, purported to have been originally written on plates
either of gold or brass, by a branch of the tribes of Israel; and
to have been discovered and translated by a young man near
Palmyra, in the State of New York, by the aid of visions, or the
ministry of angels. I inquired of him how or where the book
was to be obtained. He promised me the perusal of it, at his
house the next day, if I would call. I felt a strange interest in
the book. I preached that evening to a small audience, who
appeared to be interested in the truths which I endeavored to
unfold to them in a clear and lucid manner from the Scriptures.
Next morning I called at his house, where, for the first time,
my eyes beheld the "BOOK OF MORMON,"—that book of
books— that record which reveals the antiquities of the *"New
World"* back to the remotest ages, and which unfolds the des-
tiny of its people and the world for all time to come;—that
Book which contains the fulness of the gospel of a crucified
and risen Redeemer;—that Book which reveals a lost remnant
of Joseph, and which was the principal means, in the hands of
God, of directing the entire course of my future life.

I opened it with eagerness, and read its title page. I then
read the testimony of several witnesses in relation to the manner of its being found and translated. After this I commenced
its contents by course. I read all day; eating was a burden, I

had no desire for food; sleep was a burden when the night came, for I preferred reading to sleep.

As I read, the spirit of the Lord was upon me, and I knew and comprehended that the book was true, as plainly and manifestly as a man comprehends and knows that he exists. My joy was now full, as it were, and I rejoiced sufficiently to more than pay me for all the sorrows, sacrifices and toils of my life. I soon determined to see the young man who had been the instrument of its discovery and translation.

I accordingly visited the village of Palmyra, and inquired for the residence of Mr. Joseph Smith. I found it some two or three miles from the village. As I approached the house at the close of the day I overtook a man who was driving some cows, and inquired of him for Mr. Joseph Smith, the translator of the *"Book of Mormon."* He informed me that he now resided in Pennsylvania; some one hundred miles distant. I inquired for his father, or for any of the family. He told me that his father had gone a journey; but that his residence was a small house just before me; and, said he, I am his brother. It was Mr. Hyrum Smith. I informed him of the interest I felt in the Book, and of my desire to learn more about it. He welcomed me to his house, and we spent the night together; for neither of us felt disposed to sleep. We conversed most of the night, during which I unfolded to him much of my experience in my search after truth, and my success so far; together with that which I felt was lacking, viz: a commissioned priesthood, or apostleship to minister in the ordinances of God.

He also unfolded to me the particulars of the discovery of the Book; its translation; the rise of the Church of Latter-day Saints, and the commission of his brother Joseph, and others, by revelation and the ministering of angels, by which the apostleship and authority had been again restored to the earth. After duly weighing the whole matter in my mind I saw clearly that these things were true; and that myself and the whole world were without baptism, and without the ministry and ordinances of God; and that the whole world had been in this condition

since the days that inspiration and revelation had ceased—in
short, that this was a *new dispensation* or *commission,* in ful-
filment of prophecy, and for the restoration of Israel, and to
prepare the way before the second coming of the Lord.

In the morning I was compelled to take leave of this worthy
man and his family—as I had to hasten back a distance of thirty
miles, on foot, to fulfil an appointment in the evening. As we
parted he kindly presented me with a copy of the Book of
Mormon. I had not yet completed its perusal, and was glad
indeed to possess a copy of my own. I travelled on a few miles,
and, stopping to rest, I commenced again to read the book.
To my great joy I found that Jesus Christ, in his glorified resurrected body, had appeared to the remnant of Joseph on the
continent of America, soon after his resurrection and ascension
into heaven; and that he also administered, in person, to the
ten lost tribes; and that through his personal ministry in these
countries his gospel was revealed and written in countries and
among nations entirely unknown to the Jewish apostles. . . .

Surely, thought I, Jesus had *other sheep,* as he said to his
Apostles of old; and here they were, in the wilderness of the
world called new. And they heard the voice of the Good Shep-
herd of Israel; and he brought them to his fold. Truly, thought
I, he was not sent (in person) save to the lost sheep of the
house of Israel, as he told the woman of Canaan; and here
were a portion of them. Truly, thought I, the angels sung with
the spirit and with the understanding when they declared: *"We
bring you glad tidings of great joy, which shall be to* ALL
PEOPLE." . . .

And when ages had passed, and nations slumbered in the
dust—when cruelty and bloodshed had blotted almost every
trace of priesthood and apostleship from the earth; when saints
had been worn out and overcome; times, laws and ordinances
changed; the Bible itself robbed of its plainness; and all things
darkened and corrupted; a pure and faithful record of his
ministry to other nations is forthcoming from among the ar-
chives of the dead, to reveal the *"mystery of iniquity"*; to speak,

as with a voice of thunder, in rebuking the evil and revealing the fulness of the gospel. Such was the Book of Mormon — such its effect upon the startling nations.

STRANGE BURNING THRILLS WENT ALL OVER ME

MARGARET SCHUTT
Henvey's Inlet, Lake Huron, Canada

The following account is from Papers of Margaret Schutt Gordon, Brigham Young University, Provo, Utah. See also Claudia L. Bushman, "Maggie Becomes a Mormon," Ensign, March 1975, pages 64–65.

The first ten years of my parents' married life were spent in England, where [my father] followed his profession as a teacher. My mother's health being poor, it was thought necessary for her to take a trip or make some real change. It came to [Father's] notice that the Church Missionary Society of London sent men out as missionaries to foreign lands and paid them well. So he sent in an application and in due time it was decided to send him and his family to ... Northern British Columbia, on the northwest coast bordering on Alaska. ... So in July of 1876 we left England for a journey which changed the whole trend of our lives.

In the fall of 1877 a noted visitor came to [our village of] Metla Kahtla, Bishop Bompas, known for many years as the "Apostle of the North." He was the Church Missionary Society Clergyman in Northern Canada ... and for forty years was the guiding star of Indians and white people alike. Being the only ordained Bishop in all the North Country at that time, he made long trips visiting other Missions and baptized and ordained such candidates who were worthy of the privilege. On these trips he and his Indian attendant had to walk, ... carrying food and bedding about a distance of some thousand miles. It took six months to make the journey. Its perils and difficulties were great but this indomitable and faithful servant of the Master, with no object other than to do His service, spent a lot of his time in such journeyings. . . .

The Bishop and Mission Staff felt some system of spelling should be evolved of the Indian language and translations made and written in that, for their study and learning. So my father was given that task and because I so thoroughly knew the language in all of its system he used me to assist. . . . I would carefully syllabicate each word and help choose the spelling most suitable, then my father would write both English and Indian words, and by degrees we had the whole working language usable for printing.

[In 1882 my father] decided he would go East and seek his fortune in political fields, so we took passage . . . for San Francisco, . . . from there taking the train to Salt Lake City, . . . [which we reached] in July 1882. We had been all anticipation of our visit with our unknown relatives. . . . We were guests of Uncle and Aunt Fewson for a little more than six very pleasant months. In the late summer I started school at Rowland Hall, an exclusive [Protestant] school for girls. At the same time [my cousins] were going to the Deseret University. . . . Joseph, going about the same time I did, would often walk with me to my school and I recall how afraid I was anyone there would find out I had Mormon relations. He didn't care, but would fix me a nice lunch to take, a nice little basket, with a jar of peaches and cream, sandwiches and cake, such a feast. I recall the wonderful garden they had, the full half of the city block.

In February we went East [to Montreal, and] Father tried to make the political connections which had been promised him. . . . This never materialized [and] he had to look for employment, and after much searching had to take a school teacher job on Henvey's Inlet, Georgian Bay, Lake Huron. . . . While in Montreal, when I was seventeen, I had been confirmed a full member of the Church of England by Archbishop Bond and so was eligible to take the sacrament. I had always been a religious girl. My nature is spiritual, so I was proud and happy to receive that ordinance, and I can remember I felt quite sorry for my Mormon cousins in Salt Lake and wrote something to that effect, expressing my pride in my church. Joseph wrote back, I couldn't be as proud as he was, for he was a deacon in his church and no one need be sorry for him.

I think it was in April 1885 that a strange desire came to me, to learn something of Mormonism. I didn't like the idea at all. Brigham Young, who I was taught to think of as a wicked, immoral man, and polygamy kept coming to my mind, but in spite of my objections the idea persisted stronger than ever: "Find out about Mormonism." There was no one I could talk to, no one with whom I could discuss this strange and insistent urge. So I wrote to my cousin Fewson [Smith] in Salt Lake, saying I would like to learn something of his beliefs. Would he send me something to read? Immediately came a letter from him and some tracts, "Spenser's Letters," discussions between Orson Spenser and a minister. Every word I read was truth to me. . . . Fewson had written, "If you read this to scorn as you did here, I'll send you no more. If you are interested and want more, I'll send it." I wrote him, "From what Orson Spenser says there is not a doubt in my mind. Your Joseph Smith was a *true* prophet and Mormonism is the *truth*. Send me more." So, quickly came back the Book of Mormon and Doctrine and Covenants. My parents viewed with amusement my interest in the subject, thought it just a girlish whim. But deep in my soul was coming a knowledge nothing could take from me. I really wanted to know for sure what I firmly believed, that I had found the truth.

I decided to read the Book of Mormon first, so taking it in my hand I went into my little bedroom and, still holding it, knelt down and asked my Father, if Mormonism was really true and Joseph Smith a true prophet, to reveal it to me as I read the book. I sat down and started to read, and immediately strange burning thrills went all over my body. At first I was afraid and then a peace came over me, and all the while I read, those burning electric thrills stayed with me until I laid the book down. The next afternoon, when ready to start reading, I again took the book to my room and again prayed that if it was true I could be shown clearly. For three weeks I read each day, asking the same blessing, not realizing that I had [in my hands] the greatest converter of all to teach me. And every time I picked it up after praying would come those electric burning thrills, which I soon recognized must be part of my teaching. I never mentioned them to the folks. They never knew of the wonderful experiences I was having all to myself or how my Father was teaching me the true gospel. As I reached the end of the book, filled with the wonderful Spirit it possesses, I came to the 10th chapter of Moroni, 4 and 5:

"And when ye shall receive these things, I would exhort you that ye would ask God, the Eternal Father, in the name of Christ, if these things are not true; and if ye shall ask with a sincere heart, with real intent, having faith in Christ, he will manifest the truth of it unto you, by the power of the Holy Ghost.

"And by the power of the Holy Ghost ye may know the truth of all things."

As I read these words, my eyes were fully opened. *I gave a shout.* I knew, then, what had been thrilling and burning my whole body. It was the promised Spirit which was testifying to my soul. Without being told, I had done just what Moroni said. I had asked my father in the name of his Son to reveal unto me the truth and he did just that, and I fully knew it. I cannot describe the joy I felt. It was beyond expression. I knew then and have never doubted since, that the gospel is true and Joseph Smith a prophet of the Lord.

That spring I got my mother to read. Father would not do anything with it. She studied and we discussed it and she also received a testimony of its truth. She did not have any noticeable manifestation as I did, but she believed, and the truth came to her. My little sister also believed it. Then, of course, as there was no one we could talk to or learn from, the spirit of gathering came to us. We wanted to go to Salt Lake and be baptized. Father said that was not possible. He had nothing to do there and would not consider it at all. We thought and prayed hard. Early in the summer Mother became very ill with dysentery.... She was delirious and in her ravings would say, "If we only could go to Salt Lake and be baptized," and I can still see my father kneeling by her bed—crying—and saying if you will only get well you shall go to Salt Lake or where else you wish. She did, and then commenced plans. Some property father had inherited in England was sold and that means was used.... It was a beautiful early morning in June when we left Henvey's Inlet for the last time. Quite a lot of luggage and a little sad at losing our pets, but all anticipation of our future, in which we would go to Salt Lake and join the Church.

I Felt I Ought to Read Such a Book with a Bare Head

Karl Ivar Sandberg
Gettysburg, South Dakota

The following account is from Our Dad, *a compilation by Sandberg family members. See also Gerald E. Jones, "A South Dakota Swede and the Book of Mormon,"* Ensign, *September 1976, pages 19–20.*

The first time I heard of the Mormons was in 1923. I was then studying with a friend of mine and was reading a book about western traveling. In this book was a short account, perhaps a page or two, telling about the Mormons. I asked this friend of mine what kind of people are they? He said that they believed like the Israelites of old in giving tithes, etc., and that they had a book that they had found buried on the Atlantic Coast, where some Israelites that had visited this country long ago had buried it.

I started farming in 1923 and was batching it alone most

of the time. In the winter of 1931 I read some books that made
me very much interested in religion; in fact, by the end of that
year I was firmly convinced of the divinity of Christ and had
experienced a true repentance. But it seemed the more I studied the Bible and the more I listened to the different ministers,
the more confused I would get. I could not accept the teachings
of any church, for they seemed not to teach according to the
Bible.

One day I met a Lutheran minister at one of my neighbors'.
We discussed religion for about twelve hours. This was the
first time I had ever really talked to a minister. I especially
tackled him upon the subject of baptism, as it seemed to me
the Bible taught baptism by immersion, plain enough for any
one to understand. He offered at length to take me out and
dip me in the farmer's water tank, but by now, I had lost all
confidence in him.

In the spring of 1932 the idea came to me that if I studied
the heathen religions, perhaps I would find something that
would be better than the teachings of some of the religions I
had studied. So with this in mind I went to the free library in
Gettysburg, South Dakota, sometime in March 1932 and asked
for the Koran. The librarian told me they did not have the
book but she would send to the state library and get it. As I
was about to leave the librarian said, "We still have a religious
book you have not read, the Book of Mormon. A man here in
town tried to read it; he found it so dull he went to sleep but
perhaps you would like it." I said, "I have heard about the
Mormons but their religion is of little importance. I want to
study the leading heathen religions first."

As I was leaving the building the thought came to me that
if I was to study all the heathen religions (I considered the
Mormon a heathen religion) I would have to study Mormonism
sooner or later, so why not study it now while waiting for the
Koran? So, with this in mind I returned and told the librarian
I wanted the Book of Mormon. She told me I ought to read a
book by the name of *Brigham Young* first, then it would be

easier for me to understand the Book of Mormon. So I told her to give me both.

As I read *Brigham Young,* it seemed to me the writer had the intention of speaking as much evil of the person as he could. Many places I found where the writer contradicted previous statements in the book. This made me lose confidence in the truthfulness of his writings.

Having finished the book I started on the Book of Mormon, and naturally I felt I had started to read a book of fiction. I had not read many pages before I discovered I had found a most remarkable book and the tears started to run down my cheeks and the most sweet spirit seemed to be present. I may here mention that it was customary with me as I worked around the place that perhaps several times a day if the work was not rushing, I would run in the house and read for a while. If I read fiction, I did not bother to take my cap off, but if I read the Bible, I would remove my cap, as I considered it a sacred book. I had my cap on as I started to read the Book of Mormon, but before long I felt a man ought to read such a book with a bare head.

As I remember it I read the book in about three days and it seemed to have the sweetest spirit with it and as far as I could see the book could be true, but yet I had the feeling that by and by I would see where the book would contradict itself. I thought the book so remarkable I took it to a religious neighbor of mine and told him to read the book, but that I would have to return it to the library in three days. I felt my neighbor would be very enthusiastic about the book, but when I returned in three days, I found him scoffing at the book, saying it was all made up with a lot of names borrowed from the Bible. I returned the books to the library. All summer I often thought of the book, and yet I could see nowhere that the book contradicted itself or the Bible.

That year my brother was working for me and one Saturday evening in the fall as he was preparing to go to Gettysburg, I told him to go up to the library and tell the librarian I wanted

the Book of Mormon. The next morning being Sunday morning, as I got up I saw the book lying on the kitchen table. I
started to read as soon as I had my stock fed, and that night
before I went to bed I had read the Book of Mormon through.
I was more impressed with the book than ever. I read the book
through once more before I returned it to the library in two
weeks and by then I knew that it was true.

As I returned the book I told the librarian to write to the
state library and tell them to send all the books they had on
Mormonism. The answer came back that they had no such
books, but they sent the address of the Deseret Book Store in
Salt Lake City and told me I could get some books there.

In the following months I sent for many L.D.S. books and
as I see it now I am sure I was inspired of the Lord to order
the books I did. Naturally after I had read some books I had
numberless questions I wanted answers to. I must say that the
Spirit of the Lord revealed many things to me which I in later
study found substantiated by the authorities of the church.

The year 1934 was a crop failure and in September I hired
a man to take care of my cattle for the winter and started out
in my car alone for Salt Lake City to be baptized and stay there
for the winter. On the third day I arrived in Coleville, Utah,
just inside the state line, and as it was getting dark, I decided
to stay there for the night and drive into Salt Lake the next
morning. Being I was in Utah, the thought naturally came to
me that there ought to be some Mormons there, for up to this
time I had knowingly never seen a Mormon. So I went into a
restaurant and ordered my supper and watched the people
closely to see if I could pick out one that was a Mormon. I
may say I felt I wanted to see a Mormon rather badly for in
my heart there was a great love for the Saints. . . .

The next morning I drove in to Salt Lake City and the first
thing I knew I was driving north on the west side of the temple
block so I parked my car there and walked in through the West
Gate (I had seen pictures of Temple Block in the books I had
read) and this being Saturday they were baptizing in the bap-

tistry under the Tabernacle. The first man I met was the door watch and he told me I could not come in there as they were baptizing. (The man later became a dear friend of mine.) I told him I had come there to ask to join the Mormon Church. He told me to go up and see the guide that was talking to a group of tourists in front of the museum. I had a hard time to keep my emotions under control. I was so happy to be there and the most wonderful spirit rested over me.

I followed the group of tourists until they were dismissed inside of the Bureau of Information, then I stepped up to the guide and told him I wanted to join the Church. He looked at me rather surprised and after talking to me for about half a minute he told me to go with him to see Brother Perry, the Temple Block Mission President.... After a while Brother Perry said I could be baptized any time but being it was Saturday he asked if I would wait until Monday. Then he took the guide I had contacted and said, Brother Christensen, it will be your duty to find Brother Sandberg a good hotel and take him to one of the chapels in the morning. I spent a delightful day on Temple Block listening to the guides explaining the gospel to the tourists but under a great emotional stress, being so happy. My guide took me to the Twentieth Ward chapel Sunday morning, and being it was to be conference next week, they had put the Fast Sunday one week ahead. So it was fast meeting I first attended, and there I bore my testimony of the gospel in front of the whole congregation, after which my guide told of my conversion. How I rejoiced to hear the Saints bear their testimonies. I knew then why I had a great love for the Saints in my heart. I was at last among real brothers and sisters.

I was baptized the next Monday, being the first of October 1934.

I stayed in Salt Lake City until the 14th of February next spring, working a few days in a packing plant, but I spent by far most of my time on Temple Block visiting with the guides and tourists and attending church Sundays. I also attended night school. I was ordained an elder before I left Salt Lake City in

the spring, and needless to say I had gained a better understanding of the gospel and the Mormon people.

THE FIFTH TIME THROUGH
I SAW CHRIST'S MISSION

PAULL HOBOM SHIN
Seoul, South Korea

I was born in Korea, and when the Korean Conflict began in
1950, I fled south to escape the communist invasion. There I
met the American military and obtained a position to work as
a houseboy, which I continued for the next three years. Because
I was a displaced person, I spent most of my childhood fending
for myself. During that time I thought a lot about the pain of
life. I was keenly interested in and constantly searched for a
meaning to my life that would transcend the suffering and
make it all worthwhile.

When I first met the American soldiers who were sacrificing
their lives to help Korea, I felt that surely I could learn from
them how to find happiness and peace. Very soon I became
discouraged because of their conduct. Their heavy drinking,
smoking, profanity, and generally unloving attitude toward Koreans did not seem to bring them happiness, and it certainly
did not uplift me. One soldier, however, stood out from among
the rest. He was different. He did not smoke, drink, or profane.
In addition, he was friendly toward everyone. He even dis-
played a warm and loving disposition toward Koreans, often
calling them brothers and sisters. I was so impressed with his
life and example that I decided I wanted to become like him.

One day, I asked him why he was so different from the
other soldiers, and he told me that he was a Mormon. Naturally
I did not know anything about Mormonism, so I asked him to
teach me. He gave me some preliminary background on the
Church and then offered me a Book of Mormon. Now I am
sure he did not fully realize the limits of my language ability—

or education for that matter — when he asked me to read this book. Despite the fact that I could not read English, I admired Dr. Paull so much I determined to read the book at all costs. I took a quick ABC lesson from a fellow Korean, purchased an English-Korean dictionary, and started to read. I would read one word in the Book of Mormon, then I would refer to the dictionary for the meaning. I would write each word and its meaning down in a notebook. When I finished one sentence, I would try to translate the meaning with my own comprehension. At that time, we were not allowed light in the combat zone, so each night, even in the sweltering heat of the Korean summer, I would cover myself with a blanket to block out the light and read the Book of Mormon with a flashlight. It took me seven months to read the book once completely through.

When I finished that first time, I did not really understand what I had read. Mostly I had only connected with the continual war stories. I asked Dr. Paull how he had found the meaning of life in a book of unending war stories. He replied that perhaps I had missed the real point of the book and had better read it again! Because I could feel its importance to him, and I wanted to be like Dr. Paull, during the next three years I read the book five times, trying to penetrate its depth with my limited language and life experience. Each time I read I understood at a different, deeper level. Finally, the fifth time, I caught the vision of Christ's mission and His love for all people. I was so touched by my newfound understanding that I wanted to be baptized. In 1954 an American soldier baptized me and gave me the special gift of the Holy Ghost.

Dr. Paull, who had in the meantime returned home, adopted me and invited me to come live with him in the United States. I was eighteen when I joined my new family. Because I had had little formal education in Korea, I had to start with a GED test in order to receive a high school diploma. From a high school diploma to a Ph.D. was a long, hard road for me. During my educational struggles, I communicated constantly with the Lord, seeking His help and trying to discipline my life by practicing the principles I had learned from the lives of the prophets in the Book of Mormon. I was especially influenced by Nephi's strong faith and trust in the Lord and Alma's indefatigable courage in doing what is right. The Lord blessed my efforts so that I not only finished my education but also served a mission in Japan between 1957 and 1959. He has continued to bless my life with a wonderful family, material comforts, and many opportunities to serve both in His kingdom and in the world throughout the ensuing years.

Now, as a mission president in my native land of Korea, I continue to rely upon the verses in the Book of Mormon to inspire me and my missionaries to magnify our callings. I still find my greatest joy and the sustaining meaning of my life and its suffering in my testimony. Thirty-five years after my baptism, may I affirm to you with all my soul that the Book of Mormon is true, that God, our Eternal Father, loves all His children and that Jesus Christ is indeed our Savior and friend.

THE URGE GREW BEYOND MY ABILITY TO RESIST

JOHNNIE PHILLIP WEATHERLEY
Glasgow, Montana

I was born and raised as a Southern Baptist and even as a youth was very much aware of the Savior, who had a very special place in my heart. I was youth pastor in the Baptist church and spoke in several churches along the east coast. Friends and even pastors were encouraging me to go to school to be trained in the ministry. I felt inclined to follow this counsel, and when I started college I excelled in religion classes. My heart was behind the endeavor, but I felt something was wrong.

I was drafted while I was in college. The school had sent in my deferment papers, but the draft board never received them. So I joined the Air Force and received as my permanent duty station Glasgow Air Force Base, Montana. While stationed there in 1966, I was reintroduced to the Mormon church through a friend, Rick Rynearson, and his wife, Chris. I started receiving the missionary discussions. As I heard the discussions, many questions arose. These questions were answered by those young missionaries, even though these same questions had gone unanswered by ministers of several religions whom I had talked to. At the end of the discussions, I really wanted this new faith to be true, but I needed something more than just a desire for the Mormon church to be true.

At this time I was night supervisor in my duty section. At night, after completing my work, I started reading the pamphlets and literature that Rick's sister, Penny, had sent. At first the reading was in silence, but two other airmen under me requested that I read out loud, if for no other reason than to keep them awake until the shift was over. The more I read of the Book of Mormon, the more I wanted to read. People have told me it was hard for them to read the Book of Mormon because it was so dry and boring, but it held my interest. I could hardly put it down. Those two airmen who listened as I read were soon ready to join the Church, and they had not even had the missionary discussions.

I wanted the Church to be true because of the warmth that I felt when reading about it or when attending the Sunday meetings. But being stubborn, as I am, I had to have something specific to show me that it was the one I should follow and that the Baptist, Lutheran, Presbyterian, Jewish, or Catholic religions were not. I needed to know what made this church truer than the others that claimed to be the "true church." I felt that if the Book of Mormon was true, and Joseph Smith was really a prophet of the Lord, then I should put to the test the admonition of Moroni to ask God. If the Joseph Smith story was true and the Savior did visit Joseph as a young boy who followed his desires after reading the Bible, James 1:5 — "If any of you lack wisdom, let him ask of God, that giveth to all men liberally, and upbraideth not; and it shall be given him" — then why shouldn't I be given the assurance that the Mormon church was the one and only true Church?

As a little boy I had been taught to pray in the mornings, at meals, and at the end of the day as I knelt by the side of my bed. I had learned to pray for what I wanted and to thank Father for what I had received. I believed that if Father wanted me to have what I was praying for, then He would give it to me. If He did not want me to have it, then I would not get it. That was my relationship to the Savior: He was real but distant. I had never been taught to expect a direct answer to my prayers, and most assuredly I did not expect a visit from Him in person. Now, after having read and studied about Joseph Smith, I was ready to pray about it, and I expected an answer. After all, He promised to "give to all men liberally."

Glasgow Air Force Base is located in the northeast corner of Montana, just below the Canadian border, and is between two big Indian reservations, Wolf Point and Fort Peck. Since I was in the military, you can appreciate that I was not rich, so one of my two roommates and I pooled our money and purchased a used T.V., for which the total price was four dollars. The T.V. itself was all tubes, no transistors, and the case was made of metal. It usually took ten to fifteen minutes to warm up, and the first thing we got was sound. A few minutes later we got the picture.

My two roommates had planned to go to Wolf Point for the weekend, and I told them I was not feeling well. After trying to talk me into going anyway, they finally gave up and left me to myself. After I was alone, I knelt to offer supplication to my Father in heaven about the Church. I had decided to stay on my knees until I received an answer. I was not willing to accept a "burning in my bosom" for confirmation. I did not feel that I was requiring a sign from my Father, but I needed to know beyond a doubt for myself. I had been on my knees for approximately half an hour when I suddenly had the urge to get up and turn on the T.V. You can imagine that I tried to cast that thought aside. After all, here I was asking something that meant more to me than life itself, and I had the urge to turn on the T.V. Each time I forced it from my mind, it came back even stronger. Tears filled my eyes as I struggled with this urge. I wanted to get up and put my boot through the tube so I would no longer be tempted in that way. Finally the urge grew beyond my ability to resist, and with tears streaming down my face, I got off my knees and turned on the T.V. Instantly there was picture and sound. The picture on the screen was that of a temple built by an early civilization. That very picture was in the book I was reading, *The Trial of the Stick of Joseph* by Jack H. West. The tears rolling down my face were no longer tears of frustration but tears of joy. I listened to the program and saw more pictures, which were also in the books I had studied. After a few minutes I turned the T.V. off and lay on the bunk, exhausted.

When I awoke in the morning, everything was vivid in my mind, and I felt a newness that I had never experienced before. Yet Satan would not leave me alone or maybe I was just too stubborn, but the thought came to me that I had just dreamed it. I was sure that was not the case. Then I thought that maybe it was just a coincidence that that particular program just happened to be on while I was on my knees; and I just happened to get the urge to turn on the T.V., which urge I just happened to give in to; and it just happened that for some reason the T.V. worked instantly; and it just happened that the picture was one of the pictures in the book I was reading; and it just happened to fit in with my supplication to the Lord.

I really did not think it was just coincidence, but I also did not think that it would hurt to get a copy of the documentary so I could learn even more about this "early civilization." I went into town the next morning to the cable company and requested information about where I could write to obtain a copy of that documentary. I told the clerk the time, the channel, and what I had seen, because I did not know the name of the program or anything else about it. He checked the log and informed me that he had no listing showing any kind of a

documentary during the weekend. He showed me the logbook
that contained the programs. Nothing listed could be construed
to have been what I had seen and heard. He then told me that
sometimes the programs were preempted out of Billings, Montana. He gave me the address to write to so I could find out
what program they might have put on instead of the one listed.

I left that office knowing that the Lord had answered my
prayer. I received a letter approximately a week later from the
main cable company in Billings, apologizing for not being able
to help me but that they had no record of any documentary
of the kind I described being on the air at the date and time
I had stated.

Well, I don't need the Lord to hit me in the head with a
bat or to be struck by lightning. I accepted His answer and
was baptized December 28, 1966, in a little branch in Glasgow,
Montana.

LORD, PLEASE LET MY PEOPLE
BELIEVE THIS BOOK

KATHERINE WARREN
Hartford, Connecticut

When I was living in Connecticut, I had an opportunity to meet
the missionaries from the Church when they came by. That
was in 1967. They gave me *Joseph Smith's Testimony*. I
believed every word, and I wanted a copy of the Book of
Mormon. I told a friend of mine about it. She had one from
a garbage collector, who had taken it out of a lady's garbage
because it looked like a Bible. The garbage man gave the book
to a friend who belonged to my church. She didn't understand
it because it looked like a Bible and it had scriptures in it, but
it said, "The Book of Mormon." Several times she decided to
throw it away, but she couldn't do it. I told her about *Joseph
Smith's Testimony*. She was visiting me at the time. She said,
"Katherine, I believe I have that Book of Mormon, and you

can have it." After she went home that evening, she called and told me she had it. She brought it to me.

I started reading that book, and oh, it was some good! Before I got the book, there was something in my heart. The Lord was leading me to search. It was just something that was revealed to me. There was something else other than the Bible! When I got the Book of Mormon, that feeling left, and I knew that was what the Lord wanted me to have. I read it. One night I was reading the book of Third Nephi when Jesus visited the Nephites and told them how to baptize. I was then a member of the Church of Christ. They baptize in Jesus' name instead of "Father, Son, and Holy Ghost." I believed in that doctrine with all my heart at the time. I laid the book aside. I was in my bed, and everyone was sleep. It was quiet, and I used to read late. As I was lying on the bed pondering all of what I just read, I thought, "Jesus told them how to baptize, but these people took Acts 2:38 and baptized in the name of Jesus Christ." I laid the book aside and I said, "This is just something someone has written!"

As I lay upon the bed pondering on what I had read, I think I dozed off to sleep then. Something touched my hand, and it was powerful. I can't explain how it felt. It was just like electricity. It shocked me. I could hear a voice over my head speaking out. It was just like it was quoting the same scripture I had read. It said, "Believe all things." I felt like I was just nothing. I felt so little. I could feel the eyes of God just piercing my soul. It didn't say any more, but after it left off speaking to me, I could feel His eyes on me.

My aunt and I were living together. We had different rooms. She had her bedroom, and I had my bedroom. I heard her go into the bathroom. I was so glad to know that she was awake. When she went back into her room, I ran in there crying. I told her what happened. She told me, "Read it to me." I read it to her. She was all wrapped up in the church the same as I was. She said, "But his name is Jesus and you're supposed to be baptized in Jesus' name." I said, "No, Aunt Eva, Jesus told those Nephites to baptize in the name of the Father, Son, and Holy Ghost." She said, "But his name's Jesus." I said, "The Lord just told me to 'believe all things.'" We read that book until six o'clock that next morning. I didn't go back to sleep. It was time to go to work then. I told different ones at church about it, and they criticized it. But I still believed it. . . .

I brought my son home to New Orleans in 1967, and my daughter and I went home in 1968. We left our furniture with different friends. The Lord revealed to me to tell them, "Let's have a Bible class." This just came out, based on how large our family was. Some of my relatives came to my older sister Dorothy's house to welcome us back home. We were all talking about how large our family was. I said, "We should start a Bible class." Every last one of them agreed. "When are we going to start it?" "Next Sunday!" We started the Bible class.

I married my children's father, the man who broke my heart, and we moved. I used to go back every Sunday and teach in the Bible class. We used to go from house to house, teaching the Bible. I kind of introduced the Book of Mormon little by little. When the Lord revealed to me in Connecticut about this book, He revealed to me that everyone who rejects that book would be cast off at the last day. There is no way to be saved without the Book of Mormon. If you don't believe in the Book of Mormon, you just don't believe the Bible. I was careful about how I told them because I really prayed. My aunt and I prayed for them that morning. I said, "Aunt Eva, let's pray before we read." We prayed, and I told the Lord, "Please let my people believe this book when I introduce it to them." Some of them did; Heavenly Father was with me all the way.

After I moved, I started going to the Church of God in Christ. I wanted to find the Church of Jesus Christ, so I looked in the telephone directory. I found the ward, and I started going there. I investigated the Church for about three years. They were prejudiced in that ward. They didn't want any blacks. There weren't any blacks there. Yet I felt good when I went. I kept going, even though nobody ever said anything to me. I didn't even know they had missionaries there. I had met the missionaries when I was in Connecticut. I used to go there and sit and listen.

It was 1970 when I first started going there. I moved down here in 1969, and it was 1970, 1971, and 1972 that I went back and forth to the ward. I didn't know how to go about joining the Church until I wrote to Salt Lake City. I wrote to President Kimball. He sent my letter to the New Orleans ward. They sent the missionaries out to me with my letter. They told me they had my letter and asked me if there was anything they could do for me. I told them I wanted to become a member of the Church, and I wanted to know how to go about it. They said, "It's hard to become a member of this Church. Have you heard what Joseph Smith said, that it wasn't time for the blacks as yet?" They said something like, "If the blacks come to us, we will receive them. We can't cast them away."

They said, "But we would like to teach you." They used to come. They asked me all the questions. I knew all the answers to the questions they asked me. They said, "It's time for you to get baptized now." They gave me all the lessons in 1975. They said, "Ask your husband if you can be baptized." I asked my husband, and he told me no. They said, "Sister Warren, this is your church. You can continue to come here. It might be fifty years before you get baptized, but you continue to come to church."

I kept going to church, and they sent two more missionaries out. They taught me. They made my husband angry by asking so many questions. My husband told them not to come back anymore to teach. He told them to continue teaching me at the church. I had already been taught. I was teaching them. Those missionaries told me, "We came to teach you, but you're teaching us." The second crew of missionaries gave me all the lessons and told me I was ready for baptism. They told me to ask my husband. They wrote a petition for me to get him to sign. I asked him to sign it, and he signed it. He said, "If this is what you want, I will sign it. I ain't never heard of such a thing." I gave it to them.

The missionaries told me, "There's one thing, Sister Warren. Bishop Williams is going to have to come down from Baton Rouge to interview you for baptism." Bishop Williams came down from Baton Rouge to interview me one night at the church. My husband wouldn't let me go.

I went on a fast. One night an angel of the Lord visited me. I was about to give up on joining the Church. I wanted to join because the Spirit had led me to join, but I was having such a hard time. A man dressed in plain clothes came out of my back room. I was living on Touro Street, not far from here. He went to the front door. When he went to open it, I felt like the Spirit was leaving me. One of the missionaries was named Elder Nelson. The man in plain clothes was the same height as Elder Nelson, same size as Elder Nelson, and he had on a grey suit. I said, "Elder Nelson, you're welcome in my home." He turned and came back to the bed. It wasn't Elder Nelson. It was another person. His face was glittering, and he just looked down on me. He didn't say anything. He just took my hand and just strengthened me. He gave me strength and revealed to me to let the missionaries come in my home to interview me. My husband said they weren't welcome there. My husband didn't want them to come, but he was working next time.

The next morning I called the missionaries, and I told them to come to interview me, to get in touch with Bishop Williams. Bishop Williams and his wife came, and the two missionaries came to my house. He interviewed me for baptism. I was baptized Christmas Day in 1976. I had a time getting in the Church! (From a tape-recorded interview.)

THE LIGHT WAS SHINING ON A PARTICULAR BOOK

LARRY D. GARSKE
Cottage Grove, Oregon

The year 1968 seemed to be a critical point in my life—it was a time for some major decisions that could have long-lasting effects. I was a leader of a very successful country western band. We had been featured on local radio and television and had just been given the opportunity to audition for a major record company. Being well aware of the temptations that this kind of life would bring, I was concerned that I might be the victim of my success rather than the beneficiary, unless I could find someone or somewhere from which to draw the strength I needed. I didn't want to fall victim to the weaknesses that I had seen other musicians encounter.

I did a lot of reading on a lot of various subjects and knew that some people had a belief in a Supreme Being, but I had never really considered it seriously. But if there was a basis to these beliefs, I felt, maybe this would be a time to test them. These thoughts led me that day to kneel in prayer. It was the second day after Christmas. I went to my bedroom, and because I had never been taught about prayer, I prayed out loud. I asked the Lord to give me the guidance and strength that I needed and to know if He really existed.

As I began to pray, a feeling came over me, a feeling that I knew was from outside myself, a burning yet peaceful feeling. As this feeling rested upon me, I felt that I was being led from my bedroom into my living room.

In my living room was a large window that reached almost to the floor, and along the base of that window I had my collection of books stretched along the wall. The sky was overcast with heavy clouds, and there had been heavy snowfall all week. As I was standing there with this feeling burning within me, a ray of light broke through the clouds and a splinter of it shone on the books at my feet. The feeling grew stronger as I noticed the light was shining on a particular book. I looked at the book and felt the feeling within me. There was no doubt that there was a connection. I reached down and picked up the book. It was the Book of Mormon.

I had bought this book along with others at an auction two years previous. I had read all of the other books, but I had never opened this one or knew what it contained. I began reading it right then and there. I finished reading it forty-eight hours later—I knew it was true. The day after I had finished reading it, the full-time missionaries tracted me out. Needless to say, I was a golden contact. I had many questions, but the content of the book was burned in my soul, and I knew my prayer had been answered and that God was a reality.

MORE POWERFUL THAN
A SWORD

JOSEPH G. C. JUNG
Taipei, Taiwan (Republic of China)

The following account is from Tambuli, *February 1988, pages 9–10. Copyright © by The Church of Jesus Christ of Latter-day Saints. Reprinted by permission.*

I was sixteen when the missionaries challenged me to study the Book of Mormon. As I read it, I felt it was a good book. So when the missionaries asked me to be baptized, I did so. I joined the Church not because I had gained a strong testimony, but because I had not had any bad or unpeaceful feelings while reading the Book of Mormon or attending Church. It seemed that I accepted the gospel naturally.

But some time after I had joined the Church, I began to worry that perhaps I should not have joined a "Western" church. During this time, I did not have the courage to tell any of my friends that I was a Latter-day Saint. In fact, I covered my Book of Mormon with a piece of white paper so that no one would know what I was reading.

Finally I decided to find out for myself whether or not the Book of Mormon is true. As I was reading and praying one day, I came to this passage:

"And no tongue can speak, neither can there be written by any man, neither can the hearts of men conceive so great and marvelous things as we both saw and heard Jesus speak; and no one can conceive of the joy which filled our souls at the time we heard him pray for us unto the Father.

"And it came to pass that when Jesus had made an end of praying unto the Father, he arose; but so great was the joy of the multitude that they were overcome.

"And it came to pass that Jesus spake unto them, and bade them arise.

"And they arose from the earth, and he said unto them: Blessed are ye because of your faith. And now behold, my joy is full.

"And when he had said these words, he wept. . . . " (3 Nephi 17:17–22.)

As I read these words, I started to cry. My heart was filled with the great love the Lord has for me. I cried in my heart, "O my Lord. I know thou livest. I know the Book of Mormon is true."

Now I knew that the Church is a universal church. Joyfully, I took the white cover off my Book of Mormon.

At about this time, I also received the strong impression that I should become a full-time missionary. After serving two years in the [Chinese] Navy, I was able to get my parents' permission to serve a mission. There I had the privilege to testify of the Book of Mormon, of which I was once ashamed, and to proclaim the gospel in my own language. My mission widened my understanding of the gospel and deepened my testimony of the restored truth.

My wife and I were married in the temple. We began to read the Book of Mormon together while we were dating. We now have three children. We feel that the Book of Mormon has changed our lives completely, for, as it is written, "The preaching of the word [has] a great tendency to lead the people to do that which [is] just — yea, it [has] had more powerful effect upon the minds of the people than the sword, or anything else...." (Alma 31:5.)

A VOICE KEPT REPEATING, "IT'S TRUE, IT'S TRUE"

TROY JOHNATHON BODNAR
Columbus, Ohio

I was born in Youngstown, Ohio, on April 16, 1966, and was baptized into the Catholic church a month later. In my senior year of high school, I decided to study for the Roman Catholic priesthood. I felt that I had a calling from God for this particular vocation. I have always enjoyed helping others and thought that I could do this as a priest while bringing people closer to Jesus Christ. This truly excited me.

In August 1984, I left for the Pontifical College Josephinum in Columbus, Ohio, a seminary. Here I was to spend the next four years of my life. I had known of The Church of Jesus Christ of Latter-day Saints because my mother used to be a member. She converted to Catholicism when she married my father; however, I had and still have many relatives who are members. For some reason, I have always had a keen interest in Mormonism. I can remember doing a history report in middle school on Joseph Smith and the history of the Church, complete with a model of the Hill Cumorah.

The summer after my freshman year at the Josephinum, my aunt and her friend were going to vacation in Maryland. They asked if I would drive them, and I accepted. On our way there, I remember my aunt's friend telling me to exit the beltway outside of Washington, D.C. She said that there was something she wanted me to see. Sure enough, we pulled into the parking lot of the Washington Temple Visitors' Center. I had always wanted to see it up close. I had seen the temple from the beltway every time we went to visit my grandmother in Maryland. I had stared at it with great awe and interest and was disappointed when it vanished from my sight.

While we were at the Visitors' Center, I remember a missionary, a retiree, whom I talked with. I told him I was a Catholic seminarian but had many relatives who were members of the Church. He then asked me if I'd ever read the Book of Mormon. I replied no. He gave me a copy of it and then guaranteed me that if I read it and accepted the challenge by Moroni, I would be baptized and confirmed a member of The Church of Jesus Christ of Latter-day Saints.

Little did I know that Moroni 10:3–4 and the Book of Mormon were to haunt me for a while. I knew deep in my heart that if I did read it and accept the challenge to pray about it, I would be converted. Nevertheless, I did not want to convert. After all, I was studying for the Catholic priesthood. Besides that, I had also always been taught that the Catholic church was Christ's true church on earth. He certainly could not have two of them. Which was correct? I believed Rome was.

Every time I tried to read the Book of Mormon, I immediately closed it for fear of my conversion. During my sophomore year in the seminary, I was bombarded with anti-Mormon teachings in my classes. I did not believe most of it and even defended the Church; however, I was still a bit confused and wanted to know the truth. So, I called the missionaries in Columbus. They came over several times, and I and several of my friends had some very interesting and informative discussions. I found the missionaries to be most healthy — both mentally and spiritually. Many misconceptions my friends and I had were cleared up. Soon the end of the school year came, and we went our separate ways. The missionaries asked me if I would read the Book of Mormon over the summer, and again, I was haunted with that request and the thought of Moroni 10:3–4.

My junior and senior years at the Josephinum were horrible. I found myself being led farther and farther from Jesus Christ and the path of righteousness. I was drinking, smoking, swearing, and the like. I still wanted to be a priest, though. Something was wrong. After much thought and prayer, I decided to discontinue my studies for the priesthood after my graduation from college seminary. As a matter of fact, I was very turned off by religion. I still believed in God, Jesus Christ, and the Holy Ghost but felt that I did not need religion to get to heaven. As long as I prayed and led a good life—which I was not doing a good job at—I would get my reward in heaven. Boy was I ever wrong!

In October of 1988, I went to Chicago to visit my best friend and then to Madison, Wisconsin, to see my cousin, who is a Mormon. My cousin asked me why I left the seminary, and I told him the many reasons why. He then asked me if I would read the Book of Mormon. (Here we go again!) Once again, I was filled with trepidation. When I returned to Ohio, however, I began to read it. I enjoyed it, loved what it had to say, and had a difficult time putting it down. A couple of days later, I called the missionaries in Youngstown, Ohio. They came over and we talked. We had a great discussion. They left me so fired up. They also asked me if I would agree to be baptized if I found it to be true. I agreed.

That Sunday, I went to church with them. I thoroughly enjoyed it. It left me so excited that as soon as I got home that evening, I stayed up the rest of the night and finished reading the book that had previously filled me with fear.

I sat amazed for awhile and then took Moroni's challenge and prayed about what I had read, hoping to come to know the truth. I did not know how I would receive an answer, and I did not receive one for a couple of days. Then, finally, I woke up one morning and began with a prayer. I was filled with the greatest joy I have ever known, next to my baptism and confirmation. That entire day, it was as if a voice inside of me kept repeating, "It's true! It's true!" I even went to a Catholic shrine to pray about it, but the feeling would not leave me. It only got stronger and the voice louder.

That same book and challenge that had haunted me for three years had opened the truth unto me, gave me a strong testimony, and allowed me to receive two of the greatest gifts of Heavenly Father: baptism into Christ's true church on earth and the gift of the Holy Ghost—my right always to have the companionship of the Holy Ghost, my closest friend.

I Would Carry with Me the Manner of the Jews

Avraham Gileadi
Jezreel, Israel

The following account is from the preface to The Book of Isaiah: A New Translation with Interpretive Keys from the Book of Mormon, *by Avraham Gileadi (Salt Lake City: Deseret Book, 1988), pages xiii–xv. Reprinted by permission.*

I was born in the Netherlands during World War II. In the course of the war, my father, who served in the Dutch resistance, helped a New Zealand pilot escape to Britain. After the war, many emigrated from wartorn Europe to new lands of opportunity. Although my father prospered, idealism led him to emigrate to New Zealand. There I grew up, participating in my teens in a successful rock and jazz group. Haunted by my spiritual childhood in the Netherlands, however, I broke with that subculture, seeking again my roots as a Catholic.

I underwent a period of introspection, such as the literature of the Catholic church encourages, reevaluating my priorities and internalizing spiritual principles. Becoming religiously active and involved, I yet sensed a lack of spiritual fulfillment. Soon, Israel's history in the Old Testament became the focus of my attention. Recognizing what I believed to be a partial fulfillment of prophecy in the modern state of Israel, I felt a

desire to participate in it. In 1968, in a second, radical break
with the past, I left New Zealand to settle in Israel.

Life in Israel soon involved me deeply in the Old Testament
and in its religious offspring, Judaism. Judaism attracted me
because of the unique manner in which the Jews view the Law
and the Prophets. Among the Jews, I felt a depth of understanding that, as a Gentile, I had not hitherto known. While
the analytical manner of the Jews was to me highly unusual, I
could not fault it. It penetrated the words of scripture in such
a way as to bring out an entirely new context that lay behind
the words. I began to understand the New Testament differently
also. I saw in Jesus' parables of the two sons broad allusions
to the two houses of Israel, Judah and Joseph. I recognized in
Paul's early years as a Christian the Nazirite vow. I, too, took
the vow.

While still in New Zealand, I had determined, simply by
studying a map of Israel, to which place I would go to live in
Israel. On reaching Israel, I took an intensive course in Hebrew
and began to study Judaism. When opportunity arose, I located
at Jezreel, the place I had determined. This place turned out
to be an agricultural settlement, unique in Israel, for Jewish
immigrants from South Africa, Australia, and New Zealand. I
had worked there a year when, on visiting the library, the
librarian handed me the Book of Mormon and suggested I
read it. I declined. At her insistence (her words were, "This is
for you; you must read this!"), I took the book to be polite. I
read it out of curiosity.

The Book of Mormon at once filled many gaps in the picture
I had formed in my mind from reading the Old and the New
Testaments. Many times I experienced a sense of spiritual joy
which, I soon realized, was the influence of the Holy Ghost.
Although the Book of Mormon contained new ideas, things I
had not imagined (such as Zion on the American continent),
still I knew the book was true. The things with which I had
difficulty I resolved by praying and fasting. I was determined,

above all, to be baptized into The Church of Jesus Christ of Latter-day Saints.

To my dismay, although I pursued every possible avenue, I could find no sign of the Church in Israel. When all proved fruitless, I prayed about what course to follow. It then dawned on me that I must continue to *study the manner of the Jews* until the Lord would permit me to be baptized. Thereafter, I studied Hebrew even more earnestly. I took instruction in Judaism from several rabbis. Taking this new, though paradoxical course, I felt at peace, conscious of being wholly in accord with God's will. I saw the law of Moses as a necessary schoolmaster to the fullness of the gospel I would someday embrace. My studies took me to an orthodox religious kibbutz, at which time I was formally received into the Jewish faith. I became an Israeli citizen. I truly felt with Ruth: "Thy people shall be my people, and thy god my God" (Ruth 1:16). The climax of my life as an orthodox Jew came when I studied at a rabbinic school in Jerusalem. My closest friends were orthodox Jews who nonetheless believed, as I did, that Jesus is the Messiah.

When I had thus fully absorbed the principle behind the Jewish manner of studying the scriptures, I discovered the LDS church. I met brethren evidently imbued with the Spirit of God—they stood out from all other people I had met. There followed some weeks of intense questioning by me, rather than the regular missionary discussions. The day I was baptized I left rabbinic school—one of the most memorable experiences of my life—and entered an entirely new phase. Although I was now a member of the Church, fulfilled spiritually in a way I had not hitherto known, I would nonetheless carry with me the manner of the Jews.

IT BECAME THE FOUNDATION OF MY FAITH AS A CHRISTIAN

John Robert Harrington
Jamaica Plain, Massachusetts

My second-grade teacher, Miss Connolly, was a devout Catholic but also an educator who believed in encouraging her pupils to explore for themselves. After Thanksgiving, 1965, she asked her class to write an essay on how we had spent our holiday. In order to inspire us, she first recounted what she had done over the Thanksgiving break. She mentioned how while on a foliage-viewing trip in Vermont she had stopped to visit the birthplace at Sharon, Vermont, of the founder of the Mormon Church, Joseph Smith; she went on to relate what she had learned about the life of the Prophet, including his translation of the Book of Mormon. She suggested that if we wanted to know more, we should look at this work of scripture for ourselves.

With this as a cue, I borrowed a copy of the Book of Mormon as quickly as I could from the Boston Public Library (this copy had been donated years before by the First Presidency of the Church). After reading the introductory material and the testimonies of the Three and the Eight Witnesses, I knew that if the Book of Mormon was true, then Joseph Smith was a genuine prophet in modern times. If Joseph Smith was a prophet, then the church that followed his teachings could be the only authentic Christian church from the time he received revelations from the Lord. I then commenced reading the sacred text itself. I will not pretend that I absorbed much from a first reading of so panoramic a work at age eight; however, the book provided unequivocal answers to questions about venerable points of Catholic teaching I had never been able to accept: the sacrament was a memorial of the Savior's atoning sacrifice and not a literal recreation of that event (the dogma known as transubstantiation); unbaptized innocents did not go to a place called limbo at death but instead enjoyed the peace of God; and there was clearly no scriptural precedent for the practice of auricular confession.

Most importantly, I accepted the invitation of Moroni to pray for guidance as to the truth of the record he and his father had preserved for these times. I prayed as a Catholic would, reciting an Our Father, a Hail Mary, and a Glory Be before asking my heavenly father the critical question. I immediately felt a sensation of warmth and inner peace. By the power of the Holy Ghost, the status of the Book of Mormon as a work of scripture was unquestionably made known to me.

It required another twenty-one years before I sought baptism into The Church of Jesus Christ of Latter-day Saints, because I had to wrestle with another question: Why had God caused that I should be born and soon afterward baptized in the Holy Catholic and Apostolic Roman Church? (By Catholic teaching even infant baptism is an irreversible act.) I felt a moral obligation to remain a faithful, if secretly doubting, member of the church of my ancestors as long as it was still possible for me to aspire to become a priest. I knew that I could fulfill my calling to priesthood within the LDS church because of its practice of ordaining every worthy male to some priestly office. And so I spent the next two decades of my life engaged in three separate undertakings: studying to become a lawyer and then settling into the practice of law; learning as much as I could about the teaching of my own church and investigating which Catholic religious order might be willing to accept me; and reading absolutely anything I could lay my hands on about the history and doctrines of the LDS church.

At age twenty-nine, I found myself at a crossroads: I had a job as a lawyer that I still loved, but I had been rejected by every Catholic religious order I had sought to enter because of the uncertain state of my health. In sum, there was no way that I could ever become a Catholic priest. Through all "life's billows," my one certain source of solace was the Book of Mormon and to a lesser extent the other standard works of

The Church of Jesus Christ of Latter-day Saints. The Book of Mormon always took first place in this regard because no other work of scripture proclaims more clearly page by page what has never ceased to be the foundation of my faith as a Christian. In Peter's words of profound simplicity: "Lord, to whom shall we go? thou hast the words of eternal life. And we believe and are sure that thou art that Christ, the Son of the living God." (John 6:68–69). The only escape from my conundrum was the step I had so long delayed, a formal request to the local mission that I might receive the missionary discussions.

Within three weeks of mailing the request, I was baptized and confirmed, on April 17, 1988, by President R. Clark Greenhalgh, recently released as president of the Nephi Utah Stake. He and his wife were then serving as full-time missionaries, and they were primarily responsible for my instruction in the gospel. Seven months later, two days after my thirtieth birthday, the same gentleman ordained me to the office of elder in the Melchizedek Priesthood. I know that my father, now in the world of spirits, cannot be displeased with the choice I have made. It is my hope that I shall be able in due time to perform vicarious ordinance work on his behalf.

As the hymn says, "God moves in a mysterious way." From aspirant to the Catholic priesthood to Mormon elder, I have never felt that my Father in Heaven was not offering me opportunities to follow His way of perfection. I am a witness to the reality of President Ezra Taft Benson's statement that the Book of Mormon is in and of itself the great converter.

IT BURNED OUT OF MY BEING EVERY DOUBT, EVERY FEAR

GARY J. COLEMAN
Pullman, Washington

I was twenty years old when I began to read Mormon literature and to become acquainted with Mormon people. I felt drawn to them through their friendship and sincerity; however, my Catholic training was deeply embedded. My greatest concern was over my status with God if I should leave my former church. You see, I had been taught all my life that if I should leave that church, I would be damned and go to hell, as I would commit a mortal sin.

These teachings weighed heavily on my mind all through the process of my investigating The Church of Jesus Christ of Latter-day Saints. I had also been taught that since I was the oldest son of my parents, my example, or the error of my ways, could have a negative influence on my family. I was concerned about my parents and my brothers and sisters. I did not want to do anything that would harm their spiritual growth.

The more I studied, the more I could see that the truths of the restored gospel were not part of my former church. I struggled with the concept of a true and living prophet. All my life I had been taught that any prophet in the latter days had to be a false prophet. To gain a testimony of the Prophet Joseph Smith was a great undertaking. During my search for the truth, I was seriously considering the vocation of a Catholic priest, a goal I had contemplated for fifteen years. I had served mass regularly as an altar boy in the Catholic church for twelve years.

When I was a senior at Washington State University in Pullman, Washington, a returned missionary named John Madsen became my friend. He shared his time and literature and helped me resolve many concerns. During the summer of 1962, I read two books that opened the vistas of the restored gospel to me. In one of the books, *A Marvelous Work and a Wonder*, I was introduced to the Book of Mormon. Reading about the book but not having a copy of it was a frustrating experience for me. Inasmuch as I was working in a forest service assignment on the St. Joe National Forest for the summer, I had no contact with Latter-day Saint people for many weeks. How I longed for a copy of the Book of Mormon. I did not realize that this book would be the key to my conversion to the Church of Jesus Christ.

Upon returning to Washington State University in September 1962, I again renewed contact with Brother Madsen and my Mormon friends. John was teaching an early-morning seminary class in Pullman at the time, and he invited me to attend. I was skeptical, yet anxious to resolve my religious struggle. I began attending the seminary class with ninth- to twelfth-grade students. Some days I wouldn't attend, but the class would pray me back! The course of study was Church history, and of course, the major figure in early Church history was Joseph Smith, the Prophet. Carefully and lovingly, John and his class led me to the truth concerning prophets, the Book of Mormon, the Apostasy, the Restoration, and many other topics.

Still, for some reason yet unknown to me, I was not blessed to have a copy of the Book of Mormon. Weeks went by, and I continued to learn about the restored gospel of Jesus Christ. It was near the end of October when I received a paperback copy of that sacred record, marked in red pencil, referring me through the book from cover to cover. The doctrines were clear; my need to know answers about these things was profound. I must ask God if these things were true. I knew that if the Book of Mormon was true, all the other matters of the restoration of the gospel through the Prophet Joseph Smith would be resolved.

I remember a particular early November Friday morning at seminary when our class listened to the tape *Profile of a Prophet,* by Elder Hugh B. Brown. It was an experience I shall never forget. Everything began to come together for me. I felt Joseph Smith was a prophet, and that opened a whole panorama of possibilities about the gospel.

I knew that I must resolve the matter of joining the LDS church or leave it alone once and for all. My studies were suffering because I gave many waking hours to the pondering of religious matters. I had to be sure. My example to my family had to be based upon truth, not error. How could I be sure? I resolved to go to the Lord in earnest prayer about my struggle.

Immediately following seminary that morning, I returned

to my little apartment. I reread the marked verses in Moroni 10:4–5 and then poured out my heart to the Lord, not in the rote prayer of my youth, but as a son of God, seeking expected answers to my questions. I did ask God, in the name of Christ, if the precepts I was studying were true. I asked with a sincere heart, with real intent. More than anything I had ever wanted, I wanted to know what to do about religion. I asked about Joseph Smith. I asked about the restoration of the true Church. I asked about the Book of Mormon. I asked about the reality of Jesus Christ and his work. I pleaded with the Lord to reveal to me what I should do.

I received the answer to every one of my questions. By the power of the Holy Ghost I received the answers. By the power of the Holy Ghost I knew the truth of all the things I pondered. I felt a burning in my whole being, sweeping through my body from the top of my head to the soles of my feet, that burned out of my being every doubt, every fear, every concern. Relief and peace swept over me. I knew what I must do. I immediately left my apartment and hurried back to the little building where John taught seminary. He was still there. ' I want to be baptized, John. I know the Church is true," I said.

THE FEELING LEFT, BUT THE ASSURANCE DID NOT

DONNA CHASE
Ogden, Utah

My first contact with the Mormon church came when my family moved to Utah. I was six. I remember our neighbors coming to our door with flannel board displays and Book of Mormon stories. Their constant assault on our home soon became a nuisance. One night when we saw them coming down the street, we turned off the lights and hid until they left. In our Catholic parish there were several former Mormons who were not quiet about their contempt for the Mormon church. My

parents talked to them about the situation with our Mormon
neighbors. Soon after that we were all supplied with proper
methods for dissuading missionary conversion attempts, and
thus my family soon became heavily involved in anti-Mormon
literature.

When I graduated from high school in 1983 and encountered the struggles of college classes and athletics, I felt alone.
I had lost my stability and especially my drive. I was living at
home and attending church with my family, but everything felt
empty and foreign. I knew there was a God and had a deep
faith in Him but never felt close to Him. This was a difficult
time for me. When I was younger I found great comfort in
kneeling in front of statues of saints and reciting memorized
prayers after lighting a candle, but now this form of worship
began to feel silly to me.

I began to depend heavily upon my Mormon friends. I had
always had great friends. I was impressed that they had never
pushed their church on me. In fact, they all seemed proud to
have a Catholic friend. My friends were always patient, even
when I mocked their religion and threw crazy questions at
them from the anti-Mormon literature I was reading. One
friend's patience especially impressed me. After I questioned
her about Joseph Smith one day, she told me she didn't know
the answer and asked if I would like to talk to the missionaries
about it. I felt this was a great opportunity to ruin somebody's
faulty religious view, so I accepted the invitation.

I began taking the discussions in a member's home. At first
the experience was a nightmare for both the elders and myself.
I found that they wouldn't argue with me about silly questions
concerning Joseph Smith's "men in black hats on the moon"
or the exact location of Kolob. After a while I started enjoying
the discussions. I maintained my hard outward attitude, but
inside I was slowly being touched by the love of these elders,
my friend, and the member lady who let us use her home. I
even succumbed to reading the Book of Mormon without telling any of them I was.

I finished listening to the discussions and had exhausted three sets of missionaries and their entire supply of filmstrips six months after I started. I'm certain that my friend had given up hope on me entirely. About eight months after ending the discussions I started reading through the Book of Mormon for the second time. My first time through had not supplied me with an adequate assurance that it wasn't true. I was sitting down on my bed reading one afternoon. I remember being frustrated that 1 Nephi was filled with the phrase "and it came to pass." I set the book down and asked out loud, "Is this really true?" No sooner was the question out of my mouth than I got an answer. My body was filled with warmth and began to tingle. The thought leapt into my mind, and I repeated it many times to myself and then out loud: "It is true. . . . It's true." I sat very still on the edge of my bed and repeated those words over and over. I felt no fear, only warmth and assurance until the feeling started going away. I then began to cry, begging for the feeling not to leave. Slowly the feeling subsided, but the assurance of the Book of Mormon's truthfulness did not. I sat and cried as the fear of telling my parents entered me. As I stood up to walk across the room, I was so weak that I lay down and didn't feel I had the strength to walk. I slept there on the floor until morning.

When I woke up, I called my friend and told her. Then I drove up to the house of another friend of mine who was a bishop at the time. I told him the story, and he arranged an interview with a seventy in the ward. The bishop then asked me to go and tell my parents that I was going to be baptized. I will never forget this experience as long as I live. When I walked into the house, my family was watching *Star Trek: The Wrath of Khan*. I asked my mom if I could talk to her and led her into the back bedroom. Mom sat on the edge of the bed looking at me eagerly, as any mom would, being excited to talk to her daughter. I told her that I had been working on something for a long time and that I was going to be baptized LDS that Saturday. My mom looked as if I had stabbed her in the back. She screamed and ran to the living room crying. My dad had heard enough before I made it to the living room. He yelled, "Get out!" and pointed to the door. He told me if I went through with it, he would show up at my baptism with a shotgun and break it up, and as long as I was a Mormon, I was not welcome in his home.

I went back up to my friend the bishop and told him what had happened. We set up my baptism, and I then went to a hotel. I could have stayed with friends, but I had to make sure that I was doing this for the right reason and that it was worth it to me. Four days later I was baptized. My friend and I kept one eye on the door the whole time waiting for my dad to come in and break it up. He didn't show, and I was baptized September 9, 1984. I then moved to California to live with my aunt. After serving a mission in the Texas San Antonio mission, I am currently living with my last companion's family in Provo and am a junior at Brigham Young University.

THEY GAVE ME A COPY WITH ALL OF THE PAGES

ANTONIA PURINA HONRADO
New York City, New York

One Sunday morning, almost six years ago, I met a young man in my building on his way to church. He was neatly groomed and greeted me with a smile. I noticed a certain book in his hand. He wasn't reading it, just carrying it with a cluster of other books. Nevertheless, for some reason that book caught my attention, so I asked him what it was. He replied it was a Book of Mormon, showing me the blue cover. I proceeded by asking him if I could have it, and without hesitation, he gave it to me. Looking at his watch, he said he was going to be late for the meetings and scurried off, leaving me with no explanation of this book that caught my eye.

I began at once my investigation of this book, reading it

and pondering over its contents. It offered me something more than I had previously felt by my studies of other books of religion. I had been looking for something all my life. You see, I was baptized and raised in the Catholic Church. My parents were faithful members and taught me the ways of God, but I felt there was something missing. Therefore, at the young age of sixteen, I began my search for that something.

Attending churches and listening to their different doctrines only left me more discouraged. Nothing seemed to satisfy me. I even began to doubt my own beliefs about God and His existence. However, this new book in my possession offered me insights to such things as the heavens, God the Father, our Savior Jesus Christ, and the Resurrection. I felt the power of this book, which later on helped me to understand more about life. My studies increased, and I began to read it every night, comparing its teachings with those in the Bible, reading parts here and there.

One night, after meditating over what I had previously read in the book, I decided to apply the scripture in Mormon 9:21, which reads, "Behold, I say unto you that whoso believeth in Christ, doubting nothing, whatsoever he shall ask the Father in the name of Christ it shall be granted him, and this promise is unto all, even unto the ends of the earth." I believed in Jesus Christ, so I asked the Father if this book was true and if He could tell me. Then, I crawled into bed feeling good, anxiously awaiting the answer to my supplication.

The following morning, I woke up after a dream in which I knew that God heard my simple prayer. He really does live, and this book that caught my eye contains His word. Never before had I felt something so strong. This, also, helped me understand the death of my son that would occur months later. I knew that God lived and cared about me.

After this experience, which I call a revelation, after my prayer over the Book of Mormon, I desired to learn more about this true book. Some time had passed since the boy had given me it, and I hadn't seen him since.

I began knocking on doors in the building, asking if they knew of this boy and the Mormon church. Most of the people replied negatively, while others had never even heard of the Mormon religion. My search went on for six years to find somebody who knew something about the Mormons. Now that I look back, if I had known the complete name, The Church of Jesus Christ of Latter-day Saints, I could have looked it up in the phone book and saved me years of searching.

Not being able to find the boy or his religion, I continued on with my reading and enjoying all the wonderful truths within its pages. I never was able to read the entire book, though.

One afternoon when I arrived at home, I found out that my grandchildren had needed a coloring book. The Book of Mormon must have caught their eye, too, as they decided to mark their favorite passages. By the time they were finished, the book was colored up and ripped into pieces. The only part remaining intact was from the picture of Samuel the Lamanite to the end of the book.

For the next few years, I read and reread the books of 3 Nephi to Moroni, while continuing my search for the church of the book. In August 1988, six years from the time I first received the book, my prayers were answered again. I met a Mormon lady who wrote down my address and said she'd send missionaries to visit me. When those two young men knocked on my door, I knew they would help me come to the end of my search.

One of the first teachings Elder Claypool and Elder Jorgensen shared with me was about the importance of prophets, then Joseph Smith, then the wonderful Book of Mormon. I anxiously took out my battered copy, showing them I had a part. Then they gave me a copy with all the pages.

My joy was only beginning in the gospel of Jesus Christ. I felt so much closer to Him because of the book. Thanks to the Book of Mormon, and the clear teachings of the elders, the commandment and privilege of baptism was easy to accept. I knew it was what God wanted me to do. I knew it was what I wanted to do.

Hey, That Means I Am Becoming a Christian

Radmila Ranovic
Baden, Switzerland

While I was living in Switzerland, four young men appeared at the door. It was 1974, September probably, and in those days everybody had long hair. These young men had really short hair, white shirts, ties; they looked really weird, and they said they had been given my address. My pen pal in New Zealand had said she would be sending some friends to see me, so I said, "Oh yes, I was waiting for you. Come in."

They spoke pretty good German, so I didn't even try my English. It was really bad then. I figured out three of them were Americans and one was from Germany. They had been in our house for a while when finally I asked them, "Well, so how did you go to New Zealand?" They said, "We were never in New Zealand."

I said, "What's going on here? How did she give you my address?" And they said, "Oh, we represent the Mormon church."

I said, "What?" That was the first time I ever heard the name, and I was shocked. I realized that she'd sent me some missionaries, and I thought, "Oh no, how am I ever going to get rid of these guys?"

They were really polite and nice, smiling all the time, and they said, "Well, do you know anything about the Mormon church?"

I said, "No," and I really didn't want to know anything. It was something strange for me.

They said, "Well, we could tell you something if you are interested."

"No, not really."

They said, "Okay, well, we came just to tell you about the Church, but if you're not interested that's no problem." So they just got up, and I couldn't believe they were leaving.

When they were at the door, one of them said, "Oh, by the way, do you know who Krešimir Ćosić is?" I mean, *Everybody* in Yugoslavia knows him. And he said, "Well, he's studying in our university. I've seen him play there many times." I started to think, "Wow, how come some Yugoslav would join some weird sect like this? What is it all about?" That's when I started to feel a little curious about it. They left a pamphlet and said they would have a little movie in the church that showed something about the Mormons, and if I were interested I could come.

I went with my boyfriend. He had been in the United States as an exchange student and heard about Mormons but just bad things. He stayed with a black family, and they didn't like the Mormons at all. They said Mormons were Ku Klux Klan. So that's how he felt about Mormons, but he didn't tell me. We went to the place where they showed the film. I felt that churches were just for stupid people, but this was a little meeting room in the basement of a normal apartment building. Suddenly, on the wall, I saw a sign that said, "The glory of God is intelligence." That really shocked me. "Intelligence. These people believe in intelligence — really amazing."

They showed *A Voice from the Dust*. It was about the pyramids in Central America, and that's something I had always been interested in. They talked about the Book of Mormon, and they said, "If you want to find out if it's true, you can ask God and you will get the answer." That really impressed me. I said, "Wow, these people actually believe you can find out for yourself directly from God. I can just take the book and read it and find out myself."

After the presentation, the missionaries asked us how we liked it. My boyfriend started to yell at them and said they were Ku Klux Klan. I was so embarrassed. One missionary had been stuttering and suddenly couldn't say a word. I felt so sorry for the guy that I turned my back and stood off to one side. He saw me and asked, "Well, do you feel the same?" I said, "No, I don't. I would like to see that book." He said, "Okay, do you want me to bring you one?" I said, "Yes, can you?" He whispered, "I'll bring you one."

They came by another day and brought me a Book of Mormon and said, "We have some discussions that talk about that book, and we could teach you." I said, "No, no, you said I could find out for myself alone. I don't need you." So they just left the book, and that was that.

All this was in September 1974. I had the book till Christmas and I was curious, but I didn't do anything about it. At Christmastime in Switzerland they used to show lots of movies on TV, religious ones that talked about Jesus Christ. I remember sitting there, watching, and I thought, "I always wanted to find out more about Jesus Christ, and I never did. Where is that book? I should start reading it."

I started to read, and I couldn't understand a word. I spoke good German, but there were words I'd never heard before, like *repentance*. What does it mean? What is repentance? I was so ignorant about anything religious. Even when I understood the words, the book didn't make much sense to me somehow. That's when I finally had the desire to see the missionaries. I was thinking maybe I should read and ask them questions and we could discuss it. I still had their phone number, and I knew where their meeting place was, but then I thought, "No, I can't go there. I don't want to."

The first week after the New Year, I was home alone in the afternoon when somebody knocked on the door. It was missionaries. They were totally different ones, but I realized who they were. They came in, and I told them, "Oh, I started to read this book, but I don't understand it. I'll suggest something: I'll read ten chapters every week and write down my questions, and you can come and answer my questions." And they said they would.

I remember the first time they asked me to kneel down and pray with them. It was like something was pulling me back, saying, "Don't, don't." I was really suffering. They were already on their knees and waiting for me, and I was just sitting there, saying, "I can't do that." I finally did, though, and I had to pray, and I don't know how I said it, but it was really a weird feeling. Then I began praying for a while alone in the evenings. I would lie down in my bed and just kind of talk, like, "Okay, God, if you are there, I would like to know about the Book of Mormon. Is it true or not?"

I felt like I was talking to an empty space and that feeling was always bothering me. Sometimes I'd feel so stupid. I'd hope nobody could see me, nobody would find out what I was doing. It was really like doing an experiment. And I decided I'd stick to it, I'd do it.

The missionaries told me to pray about the Book of Mormon and read 3 Nephi. I was reading chapter 17 in 3 Nephi where it tells about Jesus Christ and that he came to America and was preaching. He wanted to go away, and all the people begged him to stay. Then he asked the children to come, and he blessed them. It said that he cried, and in that moment I was touched and I was crying. I remember it was just afternoon or evening, my door was open and my parents were watching TV, and I was lying on my bed reading the Book of Mormon and crying.

I suddenly said to myself, "You're so stupid, why do you cry about it? You don't believe that there is any Jesus Christ. You don't believe in this. This is just a fairy tale, nothing else. Why do you cry about it?"

And in that moment I felt so strongly that it had all happened. I couldn't deny it. It was real. It wasn't a fairy tale. There was Jesus Christ, and all this had happened. It was kind of a scary moment to admit to myself, "Okay, I believe now in this." And so the next step was, "Okay, if I believe in the Book of Mormon, I believe in Jesus Christ." And then, the next step was, "Hey, that means that I am becoming a Christian." It was all very scary for me.

When the missionaries would come in, I would start shaking. It was like I was really cold, so I would go and put a sweater on, and I would still shake. When the missionaries would leave I would stop. I was not afraid, but it was a strange feeling that they were bringing in, and I could feel it very strong. One time Elder McMurtry asked me, "Well, did you pray about the Book of Mormon?"

I said, "Yes, I did."

"Did you get the answer?"

I said, "No."

He said, "Okay, let me explain how the answers are." He explained the feelings that you have when the Holy Ghost tells you the truth. And he said, "Did you ever feel like your bosom was so full and you felt so happy that you wanted to cry?"

I thought, Oh, that guy knows everything. I had to admit, "Yes, I did."

He said, "Was that when you were reading the Book of Mormon?"

"Yes."

He said, "So do you believe the Book of Mormon is the word of God?"

I said, "Yes, I do."

Right when they asked me, I knew the Book of Mormon was true, I knew everything they said was true, and there was no reason why I should pray about it to be baptized. I knew that was the thing I had to do. I wanted to become a Christian, and I knew they were the ones who brought that nice spirit there that I couldn't feel anywhere else. Actually I wanted to be baptized, but just admitting it — that was the hard part. (From a tape-recorded interview.)

THIS WAS BEDROCK, SOMETHING TO TRUST IN, TO BUILD ON

Dustin H. Heuston
Aircraft carrier, Pacific Ocean

I was born on April 24, 1932, a child of the Depression, in a middle-class family in the West Bronx in New York City. I attended public schools in New York City until I was sent away in 1946 to Mount Hermon, a New England boys' boarding school that was part of the Northfield Schools, which included the Northfield School for Girls that my wife, Nancy, attended some nine years later. When Nancy and I were there, the schools still had a vigorous religious tradition that required courses in religions, daily chapel, a program of great visiting ministers delivering Sunday sermons, a series of summer religious conferences, and an inspiring sacred music tradition.

As a result of an exposure to these traditions, Nancy and I were left with a hunger for a satisfactory religious experience. I went on to Hamilton College in upstate New York from 1950 to 1954 where I received the traditional eastern liberal arts training from faculty members who worked hard to get us to think clearly, analyze well, and learn as much about the history and thoughts of man as possible in four short years. Much of their unconscious thrust was to rid us of our biases, prejudices, superstitions, and generally sloppy thinking. It was at Hamilton in a history course that I first heard about the Mormons. I remember being appalled to learn that not many miles away good people had been deluded by a poor farm boy who talked of golden plates and visiting angels. I remember marveling how gullible people could be.

I left college for a brief banking career in New York City at the tail end of the Korean War and put religious pursuits aside when I entered the navy in January 1955. After a year in various naval schools, I was assigned as naval air intelligence officer to a squadron training for a seven-month tour on an aircraft carrier in the Pacific. On the carrier I met Chuck Turner, one of the great men I have known. Chuck was Mormon and so intrigued me through his kindness, intelligence, and remarkable character that I was determined to learn about his church, which had so obviously influenced his life. For the next year and a half, I went to Mormon meetings all over the world and read as many books as I could about the Church, both pro and con. I was fascinated by the remarkable organization and the wonderful people that I met, but I was equally repelled by the stories of golden plates, angels, and Joseph Smith.

One day I realized that the Book of Mormon would be an excellent source to study, because with much of the original handwritten manuscript still available, the Mormons would not be able to change the materials to iron out any embarrassing inconsistencies. As part of my research on the book, I had the good fortune of reading Francis Kirkham's magnificent two-volume work, *A New Witness for Christ in America*. Kirkham was a humble, honest, and great writer who listed all the information he could collect on the background of the writing and publication of the Book of Mormon.

I began my studies by committing a frontal assault on the Book of Mormon. My first copy is loaded with highly charged asides analyzing every word and motive with extraordinary fervor. In rereading my comments, I am amused at my obvious attempts to unearth any shortcomings that might disillusion me in my hopeful quest. I started quarreling with the title page, was bored by the introduction, felt uncertain about the testimonies of the witnesses, shocked by the testimony of the Prophet in recounting his experiences, and totally confused by the page entitled "A Brief Explanation about the Book of Mormon."

When I started the actual prose, I was reminded of Mark Twain's comment that Joseph Smith kept himself awake by throwing in another "It came to pass" every time he found himself falling asleep. Being an older brother, I did not take readily to Nephi. Nevertheless, I settled in and read studiously and gradually began to respect the materials. After completing my first reading, I decided that there was no "smoking gun" that might discredit Joseph Smith's story. Once again, I began to visit the church and meet with the impressive people.

Knowing I was going to take another six-month cruise on a carrier, I was baptized in August 1957, just before sailing for the Pacific. I quickly found a small group of Mormons, and we used to meet every evening to study the scriptures together. Originally we had intended to study a book on the Church together, but the only volume we all had in common was the Book of Mormon. Every evening we met in the ship's chapel, which was a small curtained area amidst all of the steel.

Because we had no expert with us, no syllabus, and nothing else to do, we started together on the first sentence of the Book of Mormon and shared our thoughts, sentence by sentence. More than half a year later we had only read one hundred twenty pages, but our lives had been changed forever. For me the experience was exhilarating because I was able to bring my intellect to bear without reservation, and the book stood up to it. It is hard to express how exciting it was to be able to work with a religious document one could trust and be fed by. The previous model I had from the Bible was a group of embarrassed scholars and teachers trying to explain what was myth and what was symbolic truth in the Bible. I am and will remain eternally grateful to those people who wrote that record so that we might have the benefit of it. And as the Book of Mormon predicted, my confidence in it spread to a new confidence and trust in the Bible. Thus one book gave me two.

After leaving the navy, I went on to get a master's degree and a Ph.D. in English. I taught at the college and university level for eight years, half of them at Brigham Young University. While at BYU I had the pleasure of teaching a Book of Mormon class and was once again deeply moved by the experience of working with the extraordinary materials in the book. The next eight years were spent running an independent school of grades kindergarten through twelve in New York City. There, whenever I could, I continued to teach at church and at firesides about the Book of Mormon. The last twelve years I have been involved in working with technology and education, and although my travels and schedule have kept me from teaching as much, I have continued to study the Book of Mormon on its own terms. Like many scholars I have found that I prefer the original materials themselves or historical data concerning the materials rather than other people's interpretations.

As I studied the Book of Mormon, I began to notice that there was a consistency within the various characters that reflected not only great differences but also very realistic and true-to-life characterizations. For example, Nephi, "being exceedingly young," prayed to the Lord to see if his father's words were true, and the Lord softened his heart so that he "did believe all the words which had been spoken" by his father. (1 Nephi 2:16.) But at this time he was admonished that "inasmuch as ye shall keep my commandments, ye shall prosper." (V. 20.) Generally speaking, one can assume that this traumatic admonition to a very young boy by the Lord would be remembered and taken literally. His great test came later when he was sent back to pick up the plates and was confronted by a drunk Laban. Nephi was told to take his sword and kill him. He was reluctant to do this, but after being spoken to by the Spirit, Nephi said, "When I, Nephi, had heard these words, I remembered the words of the Lord which he spake unto me in the wilderness, saying that: Inasmuch as thy seed shall keep my commandments, they shall prosper in the land of promise." (1 Nephi 4:14.) So at this critical moment Nephi decided to keep the commandment, and he killed Laban. For the remainder of his life Nephi used the charge to keep the commandments as his bedrock. His tone and attitude were not those of a compromiser. He had had an experience, he had committed himself, and he never deviated from the commitment that he had made as a young man.

Nephi's younger brother Jacob was an entirely different person. He had an entirely different set of experiences and therefore turned out to be an entirely different person than Nephi turned out to be. I find the story of Jacob to be particularly significant not only because it illustrates my interest in the consistency of characterization in the Book of Mormon but also because it shows his circumstances. He was given a philosophical blessing that reveals some of the most extraordinary insights about eternal principles that man has ever been privileged to read.

The setting for Jacob's blessing is deeply moving because Lehi was giving final blessings to his children before dying. A man who had undertaken an extraordinary saga at such a high cost to his family, Lehi no doubt felt a need to leave behind something of great value to his sensitive child who was his "first-born in the days of my tribulation in the wilderness." (2 Nephi 2:1.) Recognizing that the child "suffered afflictions and much sorrow," Lehi wanted to assure Jacob that because of "the greatness of God," God would "consecrate thine afflictions for thy gain." (Vv. 1–2.) Drawing on his son's difficult childhood, Lehi then explained the doctrine of "opposition in all things." (V. 11.) The father was privileged to help his son to understand that all he had suffered would add to his joy, for "Adam fell that men might be; and men are, that they might have joy." (V. 25.)

At the time I remember having been so excited by Jacob's blessing that I looked forward to hearing what his younger brother Joseph would be told. I was disappointed to read that his blessing was that the Lord would preserve his seed forever. I felt poor Joseph had been cheated, but now, approaching the twilight of my life, I find Joseph's blessing extraordinarily comforting, for now I have seed.

I was interested in tracing Jacob's sensitivities in his own talks. His style is far more delicate than that of his older brother Nephi. In lecturing the men in front of their wives and children, he was very apologetic because he had to speak with "much boldness of speech . . . before your wives and your children, many of whose feelings are exceedingly tender and chaste and

delicate before God." (Jacob 2:7.) The people thought they
had come to the meeting "to hear the pleasing word of God,
yea, the word which healeth the wounded soul," but because
God insisted that Jacob talk openly to the men, he had to
"admonish" them about their "crimes, to enlarge the wounds
of those who are already wounded, instead of consoling and
healing their wounds; and those who have not been wounded,
instead of feasting upon the pleasing word of God have daggers
placed to pierce their souls and wound their delicate minds."
(Vv. 8–9.) I know of no other passage that reveals such a
sensitivity on the speaker's part to the hurt he might be giving
to the spouses and children of those being called to repentance.

As I tracked the progress of each character's life in the
Book of Mormon and continued to find that each retained a
consistency of character that often was derived from youthful
experiences, I began to sense that it was impossible for a young
man in his early twenties to write in such sophisticated patterns,
each differing markedly from the others. In fact, were Joseph
Smith the author and not the translator, his themes and characterizations would have a consistency reflecting his own experiences and characterizations rather than the extraordinary
diversity represented by the different authors in the book.

Although we can find these extraordinary differences in
the fully developed characters in the Book of Mormon, we
cannot find the character or voice of Joseph Smith. Were he
to have written the book in approximately seventy-five days,
we would find his set of themes and interests derived from
his youthful experience. They would have been alike, as well,
because in seventy-five days you do not have much of an opportunity to change. Instead, Joseph Smith's voice is nowhere
to be found.

This insight stunned me and convinced me that I was dealing with a book that was real and, more than anything else,
was a book I could trust. This was bedrock! This was something
to build on! For I, like all other people, had my own set of
experiences and characterizations, and I could not transcend

them. Although I was given a hunger for religion, I had been trained to analyze and distrust religious fervor and emotion that had caused such trauma throughout recorded history.

Suddenly finding something that I could trust changed the entire perspective of my life. At last I could let go of my doubts and suspicions about the validity of religious experiences, and I began to find my way in this new world.

I FELT SOMEONE HAD FILLED ME WITH LIGHT
LISA BOLIN HAWKINS
Amarillo, Texas

When I think back to the time when I decided to join The Church of Jesus Christ of Latter-day Saints, I feel especially loved by our Heavenly Father. He knew exactly how to bring the restored gospel to my attention. He didn't send people; he sent books. It was the perfect way to teach a girl whose fondest childhood fantasy was that she would somehow be locked in the Amarillo, Texas, pubic library overnight, and thus be allowed to stay up all night, which she was sure would enable her to read every book in the place—a goal just short of heaven itself.

I was born and lived most of my youth in Texas. My father was raised in the Southern Baptist church, my mother in the Church of Christ. My older sister and I were taken to both churches with indifferent regularity, although we spent more time at the Church of Christ because we often visited my mother's parents on weekends. My parents separated when I was seven years old and were divorced two years later. Over the years, with the help of friends and relatives, I was exposed by varying degrees to the Christian (Disciples of Christ), Presbyterian, Episcopalian, and Roman Catholic churches. The thing I liked most about any church was the music, but I also felt that other needs were being met through church attendance. I had a Bible of my own, and I read it.

By the time I was a junior in high school, I had been exposed to several varieties of orthodox religion. I continued my spiritual odyssey by exploring what my mother considered the unorthodox. I read Leon Uris's *Exodus*, attended synagogue, and considered converting to Judaism and going to Israel (about twenty-five years late, or was it?) to fight for freedom on a kibbutz. For several weeks I attended yoga classes and studied Hinduism and Buddhism. I alarmed my mother by becoming a vegetarian. This was during the early seventies, when the "flower child" culture was transforming itself into a hard drug culture, and I think my mother worried that meatless meals and herbal tea today could lead to marijuana and amphetamines tomorrow. To her credit, she was unwilling to interfere so long as the strongest potion to pass my lips was Dr. Pepper. She was relieved when I left Swami Satchidananda and returned to Jesus, and hamburgers.

My next experiment was with a group of what were then termed "Jesus Freaks." A group of about ten people, mostly high school students like me, met each Friday and Saturday evening for Bible study at the home of a pleasant woman named Mrs. Paul. So far as I know, they were not affiliated with any church. My friend Renee, who had introduced me to the group, helped me to be "saved" by acknowledging Jesus Christ as my Savior—something that was easy for me to do. Renee and I occasionally witnessed to waitresses and patrons in donut shops and similar places. We talked about Christ and salvation and left tracts with the people, most of whom accepted the intrusions of these earnest high school girls with fairly good humor.

Renee told me that the group met on Friday and Saturday evenings so that we would not be tempted to date. This was not a big problem, as the boys I knew did not seem overwhelmed by the temptation to ask me out. Renee also advised that I stop wearing makeup or trying to control my long, frizzy

hair. I should wear only baggy jeans and shapeless T-shirts, so
I would not tempt men to lust after me. Again, the men I knew
did not seem to be struggling with this problem, but it took
a lot less time to get ready for school than it did before I "went
grubby."

After several weeks of meeting with the Bible study group,
I had learned a lot about the Pauline epistles and looked a bit
like Janis Joplin on a bad day. My room at home looked like
a monk's cell. I had taken down all my posters and mementos,
fearing that they were vain. I prayed and I read the Bible even
more than I had in the past. My older sister was disgusted, not
because she was antireligious, but because this particular manifestation of my search for the truth was deadly dull. She pointed
out a few facts, like it was probably okay with God to try to
look nice, and, in return, I preached at her. But she got through
to me. As I thought about my friends and pastimes, I realized
that my life held little joy. The only things I had to look forward
to were my own death—at which time I would go to heaven,
I hoped—or the second coming of Christ. I could not count
on either event occurring within the next week or two.

Furthermore, the Bible study group could not solve my
chief spiritual problem: I had never been baptized, and Jesus
said in the New Testament that baptism was required. A minister
who visited the group said that I could not be baptized without
becoming a member of a particular church, and I hadn't found
one that I thought God wanted me to join. I had other questions
the members of the study group couldn't answer, either, things
that I did not want to "accept on faith," as they suggested.
Finally, one Friday, I told them I wouldn't be back. They pointed
out that I was sure to go to hell; they prayed loudly for my
wayward soul; I cried. As I left, I told them that if they were
going to be the only people in heaven, I didn't want to go,
anyway.

I gave up. For a few months I called myself an agnostic. I
stopped praying and reading the Bible and had a good time
redecorating my room. But finally, in June 1972, between my

junior and senior years of high school, I couldn't stand it any more. I wasn't agnostic, and I knew it. So I went back to my Bible and my knees. "God," I pleaded, "I am tired of looking. If you want me to join a church, then find one for me. I am sick and tired of all this confusion."

A week or so after my prayer, I was at work—I had a summer job as a cashier at a fast-food restaurant—when a friend from school, Ron Brough, came in to buy some hamburgers. I didn't know Ron very well, but I liked him. His family had moved to Dallas from New Jersey, and everyone at school knew he was a Mormon. When Ron came into the restaurant that day, I thought, "Mormons—I haven't checked out the Mormons yet." I didn't say anything to Ron, but next time I went to the library, I literally "checked out" the Mormons: a book by Senator Wallace Bennett, *Why I Am a Mormon,* and a copy of the Book of Mormon.

I read Senator Bennett's book first, and it provided an introduction to the Book of Mormon and a lot of information about Church doctrines and practices. It all sounded acceptable to me. Then I began reading the Book of Mormon. This was different. This book claimed to be scripture, like the Bible. To me, that involved a heavy burden of proof. I read carefully, looking up each footnote reference to the Bible to be sure it was all consistent. As I read, I copied into my journal passages that struck me as especially memorable. Finally, I reached the challenge and promise in Moroni 10:4–5.

I did not doubt that if I asked God, He would tell me, one way or the other, whether the Book of Mormon were true. And I knew that if God's answer were yes, it would cause trouble in my family and bewilderment among my friends, and it would probably change my whole life. But that was not my main concern, because I wanted the answer to be yes. I had found the answers to many questions, and I wanted them to be true. As Alma explained in Alma 32:37, I "desired to believe."

Having been reminded by Senator Bennett of Joseph Smith's experience in the Sacred Grove, I was terrified that

God might personally deliver his answer. When I knelt, after much thought, to ask my question, I first requested that I receive an answer without heavenly messengers or visits from Deity. Then I asked God if this book I had read so carefully, the Book of Mormon, was indeed a book of scripture, like the Bible. To me, the whole thing turned on the book: if the Book of Mormon were a true book of scripture, then all the rest of it, from Joseph Smith to the current prophet in Salt Lake City, had to be true, and I had found a church where I could be baptized.

God's answer was yes. I felt as though someone had lifted off the top of my head and filled me with light. I spent a long time in praise and thanks, in response to the joyous answer I received. I then telephoned Sister Margaret Brough and asked how I could be baptized, explaining that I had read the Book of Mormon, prayed about it, and was ready to join the Church. The Broughs became a second family to me. After I obtained permission from my reluctant mother and had six missionary discussions in two days, Ron baptized me, and his father, Rulon R. Brough, confirmed me. At that time, there was one stake in Dallas. Now there are many stakes and a temple.

I still consider my decision to join the Church to be the best I ever made, although almost two decades have passed. And I am thankful that the Lord knew and loved a seventeen-year-old fanatic reader well enough to answer her prayers through the medium most suited to her: a book—*the* book.

I CANNOT SHARE THE BEAUTY

ANONYMOUS
New York City, New York

I didn't really believe in anything spiritual the first time the sister missionaries knocked on my door. When I opened my door to them out of curiosity, I never realized how many inner doors I was opening at that moment. I had never taken an interest in religion. I believed in the now, in the commonplace.

I was firmly rooted to the ground. All this changed when I started reading the Book of Mormon. At first the book sparked an intellectual interest in me, and I read with a keen fascination. One evening I was reading with my usual academic detachment when suddenly, like a surge of electricity, I knew deep down inside myself that the words were true. I read in 3 Nephi 17:2–8, and I knew that Jesus was speaking directly to me, that I too had to "prepare my mind" to accept his words. When I finally realized that I held in my own hands the true word of God, I was filled with an overwhelming sense of joy and peace.

I am Jewish and am surrounded by people with whom I cannot share the beauty of what I have learned. I know that one day God will soften their hearts and they too will be blessed with the same serenity and inner joy that comes from reading the Book of Mormon. I pray this day will come soon, for it is so hard to hold so much joy within myself and not be able to share it with my loved ones. The Book of Mormon has been a revelation for me, and I bless the day I discovered it.

THIS WAS THE CHURCH JESUS WANTED ME TO ATTEND

PAMELA APRIL BROWN
London, England

Missionaries from America, who knocked at our door one cold November day in 1984, were the people who introduced me to the Book of Mormon. For eight months I had felt very elated and excited, experiencing a peculiar feeling as if someone were by my side helping me through the days, knowing something was going to happen. Would it be happy or sad? The sun seemed to shine each day, unusual for England, particularly in November.

I had always felt close to Jesus from the age of five years and talked to Him whenever I felt like it. I was christened in a Protestant church and attended a convent school for many years. The Catholic religion had a strong influence on me at the age of sixteen years. I intended to become a novice nun, but inner feelings held me back and continued to do this through life. I attended many different churches with my children, but had not heard of The Church of Jesus Christ of Latter-day Saints — although, while I was in New Zealand visiting relatives, we spent many evenings watching the beautiful sunset with the temple standing high on a hill. My uncle thought the building belonged to the Maoris.

In the year 1984 things would alter for me. After nursing my parents for twelve years in their home — my mother a psychiatric patient and my father disabled from a stroke — life became difficult, affecting the whole family. Our strength was getting rather low. I would sit in the garden by our little pond and talk to Jesus, asking Him how long this would all go on and how we could take the strain. We needed His help. As I mentioned before, the sun seemed to give warmth each time I prayed. I would thank Jesus, as I knew He was there, but it was not until I met the missionaries that I felt so close to Him. The weeks went by and, wherever I went, on trains, buses, cars, walking in towns or parks, this strong feeling came over me. I wanted to kneel down and pray. It was quite frightening.

One afternoon at 4 P.M., it was getting cold and dark. I was waiting for furniture to arrive when a knock came at the door. Instead of the furniture men, two young men stood there. I knew immediately these were the people I had been waiting for. The feeling was so powerful I felt I would explode. They introduced themselves as Elder Ahmu from Illinois and Elder Hirschi from Utah and showed me their illustrated book. I recognised the New Zealand Temple. Elder Ahmu's parents had helped to build the temple in Hamilton. His mother was born in Tauranga, where my relatives live. We talked for some time. The missionaries asked to come in. We prayed. I felt so thankful — at last something was happening. It was good to feel at peace, although the following weeks did not run smoothly.

The missionaries came each week. They showed films and

gave talks on the Book of Mormon. I found it all so interesting. They gave me a copy, which I treasured. I could hardly put it down, reading late into the early hours of the morning. I knew this book was something special. Although it was hard to understand, I knew it was right. On reading the book my whole body became so hot that my head felt as if it would burst. Some days I felt turmoil. The whole house seemed to be going round and round. I felt quite afraid. Was I doing the right thing? I prayed with all my might and strength. The tears flowed. Several times I phoned the missionaries for help. They came to the house and read scriptures or told me over the phone which ones to read. They were always a great help.

My daughter and I attended the Mormon church on Christmas Sunday. I found it all so powerful and cried nearly for the three hours. I realize now that the Holy Spirit was with me. I discussed the whole thing with my son. I was so nervous at the next visit from the missionaries that I could not attend church again. I had experienced unusual happenings that Sunday. My son cancelled the missionaries' visit, but they arrived late that evening. We discussed the whole thing with my husband and family. The missionaries left in a friendly manner. I asked if I could keep the Book of Mormon, which they agreed to.

During the few days of the Christmas period, I could only think about the missionaries, their teachings, and the Church. A few days later I left a letter for the missionaries in the church. I prayed to Jesus that they would come to our house again. I knew by reading the Book of Mormon this was the church Jesus wanted me to attend, but it was not easy. My family was worried for me, although my husband always entertained the missionaries and members of the Church. He also drove us to the London Temple, which we all enjoyed.

The missionaries did return after reading the letter. Elder Ahmu had moved on and Elder Gardener from Idaho took his place. I was pleased to see them. We continued the lessons. My daughter and I returned to church. I did not realise that the missionaries were leading me to baptism. I thought that came years later, when you understood everything about the Book of Mormon. Once again, for two weeks I experienced a very strong feeling. I very much felt the need to be baptized. I decided to ask the missionaries on their next visit. As it happened, they asked me first. I promptly said yes. My husband asked me to be careful, but I knew I was doing the right thing.

The baptism was on February 28, 1984, at 6 P.M. It was the most wonderful evening. I really felt I belonged. Elder Hirschi baptized me. Elder Gardener confirmed me. I shall be forever grateful to them for their love and patience.

How I thanked our Heavenly Father, Jesus Christ, and the Holy Ghost.

IT WAS LIKE FIRE TO ME

MARK GRAHAM
Salt Lake City, Utah

I was born in Salt Lake City. My family spent Sundays at Wasatch Springs, not at church. The Winder Ward house was at the top of our street. My little sister and I visited there to sample the refreshments whenever they had an outdoor carnival. I was considered to be a bookworm by my classmates. By the time I was ten I was an intellectual and an avowed atheist. In Utah it is hard to be ambivalent about the Church. You are usually for it or against it. Our family was definitely against it.

By the time I graduated from high school, I was convinced that the Church was the cause of most of the social as well as the psychological problems in the state. I was not a good person. I smoked cigarettes. I had a girlfriend. I was ambitious and arrogant. I was vehement in my disdain for religion and enthusiastic in my embrace of everything forbidden by it.

I had one year of college left when my girlfriend decided to go to California and join the Scientologists. For reasons not entirely clear to me, I picked up an old Bible and began to

read it. I started at page 1. I read about Moses. I went to a
drive-in movie and saw *The Ten Commandments*, with the
Oquirrh Mountains as a backdrop. I thought, if the Bible is of
any value, it must be about *me* in some way. Moses must be
an archetype of the struggle of men to renounce spiritual
bondage. I memorized poems of Dylan Thomas and the sixth
chapter of Isaiah. I did not pray; I painted pictures. I asked
questions of Moses and Isaiah as I painted and walked the
mountain paths of the Wasatch looking for the burning bush.

And I sent letters to my friend with the Scientologists—
mad love letters, painted letters, colorful letters. She lived on
the Scientology boat. They read her mail before she did. They
decided I was a PTS—a Potential Trouble Source. They were
right. They told her not to read my letters and to discourage
me as much as possible.

It was summer, and I was working for the Salt Lake City
Mosquito Abatement District. I worked with a deaf man I had
worked with every summer for five years. It was punishment
for being rebellious. We were the drainage crew and the am-
phibious spray crew. Soon I was the only one he could get
along with. He did not mind if I read.

What had caused me to begin to read that Bible? What
bridge crossed the chasm of my intellectual resolution and
allowed me to decide to just suspend unbelief? I had decided
to believe the whole thing.

Meanwhile, I had not heard from the boat in Los Angeles
for a while. I decided I would be brave. I would go there
myself. I drove across the desert with my Bible and the poems
of Rimbaud. I procrastinated our meeting by going to the Los
Angeles Museum of Art. "What if she does not want to see me?
What if she is married to a Scientologist?" I looked at the saber-
toothed tiger caught in the tarpit at LaBrea.

Finally I drove my turquoise Mustang to the Scientology
center and walked in very casually. She was having some yogurt
for lunch and was surprised to see me. "Let's go for a little
ride. You can eat in the car." It did not take me long to get

lost in L.A. But before she could go back to Utah, she had to get all of her belongings. She was terribly afraid because of the tight security and the pressure she had been put under to stay. We walked into the place together. Before she could leave, they had to interrogate her. They did not like me very much. They wanted to test their mental powers against me. I could tell by the way they were staring at me. I felt peaceful. I walked over to the courtyard where I could see the palm trees. And I thought about the Savior. I felt a little of His peace, as if He wanted to demonstrate for a moment that He was able to secure those who were His.

The Scientologists tried to follow us along the astral plane, but they were no match for my Mustang.

During the winter I finished college. I was happier than I had been since I was a child. I took a dancing class and read Henry Miller. I painted pictures about the Bible. I painted pictures about things I did not even know yet; there was more in the pictures than I put there! Premonitions. When I thought seriously I was full of ideas, wonderful ideas, like a painting called Baptism. Or a painting about Moses and his bride leaving the world of spiritual darkness, dancing down the aisle as the movie loomed behind them. We lived on Center Street, below the capitol.

After graduation in 1973, I worked for Mosquito Abatement one last summer. I had an idea that we should go to New York. It was not something I decided after many deliberations; I just knew it. I also stopped at Temple Square one afternoon after work and picked up a blue paperback Book of Mormon. I read it in the back of the drainage truck. The people at Mosquito Abatement were wondering what was happening.

I did not pray about the book. I knew it was true as soon as I read it. It was just like the Bible, except pure and clear, more explicit. It was like fire to me. I felt like God had a work for me to do. A strange thought. I was going on a journey someplace I had never been before. There were no boundaries, no road marked out for the artist. I could understand how Lehi felt. By the time the stake missionaries stopped by, I had read the Doctrine and Covenants and the Pearl of Great Price.

I did not want to go to church. I did not think it was necessary. I argued with myself on the way to work about this. I lost the argument. That was how the stake missionaries found us. They were a married couple. He was a retired steelworker. He did not look like Nephi or Alma. I took a long walk up into the foothills. What was to be done about these people? They were coming over again, in the evening. I decided to receive them like, well, like angels. That made all the difference.

We went to church a few times before going to New York. Young couples asked us if we wanted to come over some time and play games. "Play games? And eat marshmallow popcorn and pink punch too, I bet. No, thanks, we don't play games. We're artists."

After the interview for baptism we decided to get married. We were married by the bishop in his office late one night. We went to Harmons for dinner on our wedding night. Two days later I was baptized at the Tabernacle. The next day we left for New York with all of our belongings. But that is another story.

As If Touched by a Magician's Hand, She Changed

Patricia Morán
Carlos Paz, Argentina

It was a hot afternoon in 1988 in the city of Carlos Paz. My companion and I decided to visit a reference given to us by a sister member. After looking for a long time, we did find this very special family, consisting of a couple and the husband's mother; their children didn't live at home anymore. The husband had larynx cancer and spent a lot of time in bed, depressed and with hate towards God for the "punishment" He had given him. All the resentment had been transmitted to his wife. His mother was also ill. She was in an orthopedic bed, unable to move. She was very Catholic and accepted her burden; she had faith in many saints.

What frightened us or, better said, what hurt us was to see Cora, the wife, transformed, grieved, afflicted, and so very angry with God. She couldn't understand the Lord's love as it was expressed in her husband and mother-in-law. She didn't accept us well. Further, she shouted at us and made us feel terrible. Even though we tried to uplift her with our testimonies, she wouldn't listen to us. Her ears were closed, as was her heart. I felt so frustrated and powerless that I could only take her hands into mine, listen, and cry with her. This calmed her down a little. I remembered in that moment what Alma teaches us in Mosiah 18:9: "Yea, and are willing to mourn with those that mourn; yea, and comfort those that stand in need of comfort."

I spoke a few words and asked her to read from the old and damp Book of Mormon that she had had for a long time. Again, she didn't listen. She left us. We marked some scriptures and left the book on the table. Saddened, we left the house. That night, I asked my Father with all my strength that she could find peace in her soul and read the Book of Mormon. I did this for a week but then forgot the whole matter.

Close to a month later, we were walking along the downtown streets of Carlos Paz when a woman stopped me. My companion didn't see her and kept on walking. To my surprise, it was Cora, but so different. In her eyes there was a new brightness. With a gentle voice, she said, "I've been looking for you for a long time. I read the Book of Mormon and my life changed. Can you see it? There's peace in me. I need to talk to you."

My heart beat quickly, and my imperfect mind was confused. I couldn't understand such a change in a woman. We arranged a date for two days later. That day arrived and I went first up the stairs of a typical house in the area (all upstairs). There she was, crying desperately, but meek and submissive, willing to do what the Lord had asked her. She opened up and began to tell us that her husband, the one who taught her to hate God, had begun to take part in charismatic meetings and, in between prayers and rosaries, hit and insulted her. He even spit on her, the one who took care of him and comforted him in times of physical and spiritual pain. She couldn't understand the god her husband had accepted. The only way out was the Book of Mormon. It brought peace, comfort, and hope to her life. Her great wish was to know if God could forgive her and if He loved her.

I understood how God works, how He used the opposition in His favor. Satan used her husband to keep her away from the Lord, and He, the Lord, used the same means to bring her closer to Him. I hope her husband will understand these things in the future.

So, there she was, crying on my shoulder, waiting for me to say something. I didn't know what to say. I just prayed in silence that the Spirit would tell me. She then told us that there was something I said in our first visit that touched her heart: "Don't say that God doesn't exist because He doesn't listen to you. What happens is that *you* don't listen to Him."

In tears, she asked me to teach her how to listen to God. So, we did. We explained to her how to pray and how our Heavenly Father answers our prayers. We recommended that she continue reading the Book of Mormon and go to church. Later we would explain the "magic book" that changed her. What I didn't tell her was that I wouldn't see her again because I was finishing my mission in a couple of days.

Not only had something in her inner self changed, but something in me did also, and the responsible factor was, as we know, the Book of Mormon. I understood the special spirit, or the special power, that it possesses. I know it's not us, nor our great spirituality, that makes the people accept the gospel. If it were like that, their conversion wouldn't be stable or secure, although our spiritual power is essential. The Book of Mormon is what works, touches, and transforms. Cora is a great example. In my eighteen months in the work, I never saw anyone so irate, so hateful, and so pained against God. So, as if touched by a magician's hand, she changed. But, it wasn't us, the dedicated missionaries who were there, but the spirit of the Book of Mormon that reached Cora's heart and surely will reach millions of other Coras. (Translated by Tomâs F. Lindheimer.)

MY BODY SEEMED TOO SMALL FOR MY SOUL

YVONNE WILLIAMS
Loriente, France

I was born and raised mostly in France, but because my father was an officer in the French army, I spent four years of my youth in African countries. My parents were practicing Catholics and had seven children. I am the youngest. They lost their second child, an infant son, in the country of Mali, where he had been born. Our family life was, to say the least, difficult. Showing any sign of affection was taboo. We had to be strong "little soldiers." People didn't speak and communicate in my family; they yelled and insulted. My father's harshness, violent temper, and domineering ways seemed too much to bear at times. We truly feared him!

I spent many hours as a child trying to figure out eternity and God. Invariably, I became very frustrated at my inability to do so. Fear would overwhelm me, and the tears would start rolling down. I realized when I was six or seven how ignorant I was. While standing in the middle of the street one day, I looked around me and saw a world I knew nothing about. I didn't know how the street under my feet had been made. I didn't know how the houses had been built. I didn't know where the electricity I used every day came from, not to mention the trees and the grass! I didn't know why God was so angry at us that He hadn't talked to us in two thousand years.

I didn't know why I existed. I stood there panicked, and I burst into tears.

The nuns of the private Catholic schools I attended tried to instill in me a good set of values. I didn't rebel against these values, but I found the doctrines of the Catholic church more and more difficult to accept. By the age of fourteen, I wondered if my rebellion was triggered by the doctrines themselves or by my parents. I decided to judge the faith on its own merits, and to accomplish this, I enrolled in a Catholic youth movement. The experience lasted a year and was a disaster. By the age of fifteen I didn't know if God existed or who was Jesus Christ, and I didn't care to know anymore!

About a week after I officially quit the youth organization, my older brother, who was twenty-three at the time, died in a car crash. I received the news of the accident around 10 P.M. My parents were spending the weekend in their summer house on an island off the coast of my hometown. They didn't have a phone and couldn't be reached. My other sister and brother had gone to a party but hadn't told me where. I felt overwhelmed with grief and so incredibly alone. I loved my brother but had never told him so. No one ever said the word *love* in my family.

At first, I started to clean the house to try to not think. It didn't work, so I gathered all the pictures I could find of him and sobbed hysterically. Then I started to fear for him. Where was he? Was he alone? Was he in Paradise? What was Paradise like, anyhow? Did he know anybody there? I couldn't answer any of my questions. In desperation, I knelt and begged God to accept him, to reassure him. I stopped praying when I became aware of presences around me. I couldn't see them, but I felt many people in the room with me. Voices in my head were telling me, "We were there when he came. We welcomed him. Please don't worry. He is fine." Among the presences I soon discerned my grandfathers, the brother who had died as an infant, and many other friendly people. I couldn't tell who the others were, but I somehow knew that they knew me and

were close to me. When I realized that I was having a conversation with "dead people," I became frightened and left the
room quickly. Later during the night the thought that there
was something that I should do for my brother kept coming
to me. I kept rejecting it, telling myself over and over again
that he was dead, out of my reach, dead.

I broke the news of his death to my sister and brother
around 6 in the morning when they returned. My parents were
finally reached close to noon that day. I didn't speak to anybody
about "the people." It was contrary to what I had been taught.
I told myself that I had probably made it up in my grief. I felt,
nevertheless, a peace in my heart during the next few days. I
was confronted during that period with some more doctrines
I found impossible to believe. I had decided that I believed
in God after all, but for the first time I realized that I could
believe in Him and not in the church I had been raised in.
The two became very distinct to me. I informed my mother
shortly after my brother's death that I didn't consider myself
a Catholic anymore.

Summer was beginning, and I joined my parents on the
island. The girls in the family received the message from my
father that it would have been different if one of us girls had
died instead. Boys carry the name. Boys are important. My
father seeemed to be taking his grief out on us. . . . I became
consumed with hate for him, thought of killing him, and then
judged and condemned myself. I was a big nobody, and I didn't
deserve to live. I started collecting pills, any pills that could
harm me. My plan was to collect enough of them to do the
job right the first time.

One day, as I was staring at my collection of pills to see if
I had enough, I suddenly felt the "inside" of me. I could see
that deep down, way deep down, I was made of love. Maybe
in a different environment I could reach down to that love and
bring it up. A small, small voice was telling me to hang on, to
give myself a chance. I threw the pills away. For the next four

to five months, I waited. I didn't know what I was waiting for, but I knew I had to wait; something was going to happen.

One day I was looking in the encyclopedia under "Mormon." There was so much in the press about the Osmond brothers being able to have twenty-four wives each, because they were Mormons. How sick! I didn't know what a Mormon was. My mother was in the room at the time, but she said nothing. A few days later, she was standing at the kitchen sink when I came home from school. On the table was a strange-looking book. Two missionaries had left a Book of Mormon with our parish priest that same week. She had mentioned to him that I had complained that our encyclopedia was too small and didn't say much about Mormons. The priest lent her the book for me. To this day, my mother doesn't remember this happening. She was so upset when I joined the Mormon church that she completely blocked these events out of her memory. I took the book, thinking, "No way am I going to read this boring-looking book!" Who would have thought that there actually were Mormon missionaries in my little French town? And what were they doing there anyway?

I had just turned sixteen. My heart was so heavy and full of anger and sadness. My father's behavior was not improving, and now my brother and sister were increasing their drinking also. A few years later, my sister would die from it. I could see my family going through a lot of pain and destruction and was powerless to help. All I could do was watch and wait.

That night I took the book to bed with me, thinking that if I read in it a little, it would bore me so much that I would fall asleep faster. First I read the Joseph Smith story, then the thirteen Articles of Faith. At the end of the book was a list of commonly asked questions about religion and where to find the answers. They were *my* most common questions! I started to read the references. It is difficult to describe what happened next. I couldn't believe what I was reading. These answers made so much sense!

As I read, the tears started rolling down. I couldn't stop

reading and crying. I then felt my mind opening up. I received a very clear vision of what was expected of me, who I was supposed to become. I can't describe the pain I felt when I realized how far from my potential I was and how much work was needed. I cried out to God to forgive me. I didn't believe that I could ever become the person He wanted me to be. That feeling of total despair was soon followed by one of complete love and acceptance. My body seemed too small for my soul. I was loved and accepted by my God! It would take time and effort on my part to grow, but I could do it. He trusted me, and He would be there to help me become what He knew I could become, if I let Him. I couldn't cry anymore. I just lay there, immersed in that divine love and responding to it.

The morning came very fast. I hadn't slept at all during the night. I felt very weak and out of breath as I prepared myself for school. I placed the book on a shelf very carefully. I think I was almost afraid to touch it that morning. I knew something incredibly powerful and "out of this world" had happened to me, but I didn't understand it. God wasn't supposed to talk to people anymore. . . . How could this happen? Why me? If me, then why not everybody else? I hadn't done anything special to deserve this.

I passed my father in the hall. All the hate I had for him was gone. In my heart I had instead a very sweet, penetrating feeling. It was so sweet that it hurt. He yelled something at me, but I couldn't get angry. All I saw was a very sick, very hurt man. I felt for him. It didn't matter if he didn't love me. It didn't matter if no one on the earth loved me. I was loved beyond measure by God! I couldn't move fast or speak very much. It took a lot of effort on my part to respond to people. At school, tears came to my eyes when I saw the priest who taught us catechism enter the room. I had been so hostile to that poor man! I was angry at him for not having the answers to my questions. Now I realized that he was a good man trying to do the best he could to teach us about faith. He couldn't tell us what he didn't know. We became friends that day.

The sweet, painful feeling remained with me two to three weeks. I wanted to keep it forever and get rid of it at the same time. I didn't read in the Book of Mormon anymore: I was too scared to open it. I went back to mass for a few Sundays, but I honestly couldn't feel God there, so I stopped. I read everything I found about the Mormons in all the libraries of my hometown. Most of it was not flattering. I couldn't reconcile what I was reading with the spirituality of the Book of Mormon.

After four months or so, as I was walking downtown with my best friend, I saw two strange-looking men on the sidewalk selling books. Next to them was a big picture I had seen in the Book of Mormon. With my heart pounding, I approached them, bought a book, and left quickly. I related to my friend what had happened to me that night and asked her to take the book and read it. She didn't think too much of it at the time, but she too found her way into the Church eventually.

Almost a year had passed since I had read in the Book of Mormon. One day, I finally decided that I needed to know more about it. I had never spoken to a Mormon in my life, and the thought of doing so was terrifying. If I wanted to learn more, I had to ask them to teach me. I had read everything in town about that church, and I couldn't bear to stay in my ignorance any longer. On Sunday morning, December 1, 1974, I knocked at the door of the meeting house, accompanied by my friend. It was a small apartment above a bar. The missionaries lived in it, and the dozen or so members met in the living room. We asked if we could attend the meeting and sat next to the exit, just in case! We were shaking from head to toe.

I was baptized, a year later, the week of my eighteenth birthday. One of the missionaries who had welcomed us to the church meeting on that first day came back after his graduation from Brigham Young University and proposed to me. We were sealed in the Swiss temple and now have two children.

My parents' initial hostility toward the Church subsided with the years. Under the prompting of the Holy Ghost, I was able to know how to reach my father. He responded to me a

year or so before his death. On his nightstand he kept a Book
of Mormon and *The Restored Church,* by William E. Berrett.
One of my sisters and two nieces joined the Church in France,
and I have over the years become familiar with many of the
unknown, friendly presences.

THAT'S WHEN MY LIFE
STARTED CHANGING

MYRTLE FRANCIS
Antigua, Barbados

In 1988 Elders Webb and Moore from The Church of Jesus
Christ of Latter-day Saints first visited me at home with what
they called the restored gospel. I had never heard about this
church before, and neither had I ever heard about the Book
of Mormon—which was said to be another testament of Jesus
Christ. Though I could not invite them in the first time because
I had a terrible toothache, my curiosity was aroused, so I asked
them to come back at a later date.

As the elders taught me the restored gospel, I became more
and more interested in what they had to say, though I did not
believe their teaching. Their doctrine was so different from
anything I'd heard before. I kept on saying to myself, "Don't
be fooled by them, Myrtle. They're just another false religion."
After a few visits the elders gave me the Book of Mormon and
suggested that I read it and pray and ask God if what I read
is true. Little did I realize then what a big difference this strange
book was going to make in my life.

Let me point out here that I was raised in a Christian home.
I went to a Christian school and was baptized in a Baptist
church. I was taught the Bible at home, at church, and even
at school. I thought that the doctrine of the Mormons was false;
I thought so because their teachings were not consistent with
what I had learned as a child.

The elders kept on teaching me, though I was not receptive

to the teachings of their church. I admired their faithfulness and the enthusiasm with which they taught the Bible. There were times when they'd come home for weeks and could not find me there, but they kept coming. I gave them a very hard time, but in spite of everything they were not discouraged.

Thank God I was open-minded enough that although I was convinced that their doctrine was false, I still welcomed them at home and kept on reading the Book of Mormon. After reading the book for about three weeks and praying, beseeching God to tell me if the book was true, I became convinced that a book as precise and accurate as the Book of Mormon could not have been written by a mere man. That's when I came to the realization that it is the word of God and consequently the church that used it the true Church—because no other church had the Book of Mormon. I then decided that I wanted to be part of that church.

That's when my life started changing. My friends thought I was crazy, my family thought I was in need of prayer, my co-workers thought there was some man in the church that attracted me. It's amazing how fast someone's life can change. Instead of being one of the crowd, I became the odd one. There was not one day that I was not reminded of my decision to join the so-called Mormonites.

The elders told me that one of the steps to salvation is baptism and that though I'd accepted the truth, I still needed to be baptized. I wanted to be part of the true Church, but I was still very reluctant to get baptized, partly because I had already been baptized in a Christian church and partly because of my friends and family. I struggled within myself night and day. I asked God to give me the courage to be baptized, because I knew that it was the right thing to do. After much prayer and a lot of encouragement from the elders I decided to be baptized.

The two weeks that followed were a very trying time for me. I had to deal with all sorts of criticism about the Church and my motives for wanting to join the Church. The hurtful part about all this was that these remarks came from people I thought were my friends. I was seized by a feeling of uncertainty. Was that what I really wanted to do? Could I deal with the criticism? A part of me wanted to go forward and be baptized. The other part wanted to forget the whole thing. The elders kept on encouraging me—one of the things they said that kept ringing in my mind was that I am the only one answerable to God for my actions. I then resolved that I would be baptized, no matter what anyone had to say about it.

I'll never forget the day I was baptized. It is one of the most memorable days of my life and one of the happiest. In spite of everything I've gone through since I decided to join the Church, I don't regret my decision to follow in the pathway of God—not even for one moment have I regretted it. My only regret is that my friends and family have not come to know the truth as I did. I'll always be grateful to the elders who introduced me to the restored gospel. I hope that one day I'll have the pleasure of leading someone to the fold of God.

IN SPITE OF MY PAST, GOD CARES ABOUT ME

EMMA J. CARPENTER
Wellsboro, Pennsylvania

When I was about eight years old, I began to wonder why we didn't have prophets on the earth like we read about in the Bible. My family attended the Baptist church, so I asked my Sunday School teacher about it, and each time she told me she didn't know. I asked her, "Doesn't Jesus love us as much as He loved those people?" She told me it didn't make any difference; we have the Bible and that's enough. It wasn't enough for me, but she told me to stop asking and not even to think about it anymore.

By the time I graduated from high school, I was having all sorts of doubts about myself and life in general. I wondered

if there was a purpose to life. I wanted more specific direction.
I began to wonder if maybe one of the other churches in town
might better meet my needs.

In 1970 the missionaries came to our home. They were
talking to my mother about the Articles of Faith on a card they
had. I was working in the next room, and something they said
caught my attention. I went in and asked if I could read their
card. I read the thirteen Articles of Faith and told them that
everything on that card was what I had always thought should
be true. Of course, the missionaries began teaching me the
discussions. They told me about the Prophet Joseph Smith and
President Joseph Fielding Smith, who was the president of the
Church at that time. They said these men were prophets. I
asked them if they were prophets like Moses, and they said
they were. They showed me pictures of Joseph Smith and
President Smith, and I remember the warm, comfortable feeling that came over me. I thought, Yes, this could be true.

Eventually the missionaries asked me to read the Book of
Mormon and to pray about it. By that time I knew I had to
know for sure. I knew it was either right, and I would have to
go with it 100 percent, or it was very wrong, and I would get
as far away from it as possible. So I said that I would do as
they asked.

Throughout my life I had said my prayers regularly and I
believed in God. But I guess I had just said my prayers without
expecting answers, especially not tangible answers, because I
couldn't imagine how my prayer would be answered. I was
afraid I wouldn't recognize it. One evening when I was home
alone, I went to my room to read the Book of Mormon. I knelt
down by my bed and asked our Father in Heaven to please
let me know, in a way that I would understand, if the Book of
Mormon is true, and if so, I would also know the Church is
true, and I would be baptized. I promised Him that I would
change my life and be obedient to the teachings of the gospel.
And if it wasn't true, I also wanted to know, because the opposition was very obvious to me. I could see only black and

white—there was no gray. I knew the answer would change my life.

I sat on my bed and began to read very intently. After I had read just a few pages, very clearly into my mind came the words, "It's true, it's true, it's true." Just as distinct as the words were in my mind was the feeling in my heart that the Book of Mormon is the word of God. I felt that excitement that we feel when the Holy Ghost bears witness to us. Suddenly it seemed as though the windows of my mind were open, and my world was full of hope and confidence.

For the first time in my life I had prayed with real intent, and God had heard my prayer. Also for the first time I knew that our Father in Heaven is real and that He knew who I was and, in spite of my past, He cared enough about me to answer my prayer.

My family had attended church regularly since I was a child. Although those churches don't have the answers to all that we need to know to return to our Heavenly Father, I was taught the basics. I believed in God, and I knew that his Son Jesus Christ came to earth to save us from our sins. I knew the Bible was the word of God. I knew that as Christians we should live good lives. Those teachings prepared me to receive the fulness of the gospel when I heard it. Now, after reading the Book of Mormon and receiving the answer to my prayer that the truth has been restored to the earth, I had the peace of mind that I had been hoping for all of my life.

Consequently, I was baptized, and I have continued to read and study the Book of Mormon. I find answers to my questions in the Book of Mormon, and reading it over and over strengthens my testimony. Its teachings provide guidance for my life. But most of all, I know that I am being obedient to the counsel the Lord has given to His people down through the ages to study the scriptures and make them part of their life.

Once, in search of a scripture to express my thoughts, I found this in Alma 39:17: "Behold, you marvel why these things should be known so long beforehand. Behold, I say unto you, is not a soul at this time as precious unto God as a soul will be at the time of his coming?" Although Alma was referring to the people who lived before and at the time of Christ, that scripture is also the answer to my childhood question, "Doesn't God love us as much as He loved the people we read about in the Bible?"

I READ IT ALL IN ELEVEN HOURS, THE HOLY GHOST PUSHING ME ON

ALEXANDRE MOURRA
Port-au-Prince, Haiti

My father came from Bethlehem in what is now Israel, but he moved to Haiti, where he made a modest fortune in the mercantile business. I was born in Santiago, Chile, but as a baby I was taken back to Haiti, where I grew up. My native language and culture are therefore French. When I was still a young man, my father returned to Bethlehem with our entire family, for reasons of health, and he died there shortly thereafter. So, at the outbreak of World War II, I enlisted in the British army and saw savage military action in Lebanon. Shortly thereafter I married and returned to Port-au-Prince, where I have remained in the mercantile business ever since.

I had never been able to settle on any particular religion, although I tried many of them. I am recorded as one of the founding fathers of the Rosicrucians here in Haiti, but soon abandoned them. I then drifted from sect to sect, including the "Science of Mind," Freemasonry, and spiritualism. As a spiritualist I succeeded in conversing with departed beings, one of whom appeared as an angel of light. But I found myself in conflict with this personage, and I now realize that it was from the evil one.

I spent many months and years fervently praying to the Lord to send me the truth. My prayers were always addressed to God the Eternal Father, in the name of His son Jesus Christ.

Then, one day while in my store, in the year 1976, I felt prompted to call on my cousin, who had a store not far away. His cousin's wife was there reading the Book of Mormon, about which I knew almost nothing. I asked to borrow it but was refused. She wanted to finish reading it herself, but she gave me a tract on the Prophet Joseph Smith's own story, which I read avidly. I felt immediately in my heart that this told a true story. I wrote to the headquarters of the Florida Mission for a copy of the Book of Mormon, but for three weeks I received no answer. I wrote again and sent a photograph of myself along with my letter. Soon I received both an English and a French copy of the Book of Mormon. I started immediately to read the French copy.

No sooner had I started than I became overpowered by a strong conviction that the book was the word of God. I couldn't put it down. I read the entire book without stopping—from 5 P.M. to 4 A.M. The Holy Ghost helped me read that book—it kept pushing me on. Tears were flowing down my cheeks. I read with understanding in eleven hours. I knew the book was true. I accepted without question the major thesis of the book, the sacred and divine mission of the Savior Jesus Christ and His Messiahship.

For the first time, I felt Jesus to be a reality, a living person, instead of an idea from theology. I felt the spiritual power of the book and its absolute truth. I had no question at all in my heart. After my long wanderings through the mysteries of the occult, I had at last found the truth. My prayers had been answered. I applied immediately for baptism. I had to go to Florida, because no one in Haiti had the right authority. When I walked into the office of President Millet of the Florida Fort Lauderdale Mission, I was still smoking four packs of cigarettes and drinking twenty-five cups of coffee a day. President Millet told me about the Mormon views on such subjects. So I threw my tobacco into the wastebasket, and from that day on to this I have not smoked a single cigarette nor drunk a single cup of coffee.

I am grateful that I have served in the Church in my country and was able to meet President Spencer W. Kimball, who twice thanked me for my faithfulness and other times sent me gifts as a token of his love. Since receiving the Holy Ghost I have been blessed with the gift of discernment and the gift of healing. I have been able to cast out evil spirits, to heal the sick and the weak, and to make prophecies about the work among my people. (From an oral interview translated by David S. King.)

I Am Amazed Our Lord Has Granted Me So Much Knowledge

Lillian E. Olden
Vincennes, Indiana

Over the last fifteen years I've been studying revelation as presented in the *Urantia* book. I joined the Society of Friends six years ago. I'd been praying that our Lord would tame me and teach me, placing myself under His care in joy and gratitude.

While searching for something else to read at my friends' with whom I stayed in October 1988, the bright blue cover of the Book of Mormon stood out among the other books on the shelf; and I joyfully took it, thinking to myself I'd always wanted to know its contents ever since I'd heard of it in high school history.

I spent the next month reading it cover to cover, while checking the phone directory to see if The Church of Jesus Christ of Latter-day Saints was here in Vincennes. Because weeks passed before circumstances could get me in touch, I knew our Lord would answer me in the form of a person. I met her within a week of my receiving this knowledge, and she took me to the meetinghouse the next Sunday.

I was deeply touched by the follow-up visits by the missionary elders and the friendship and lessons of the members. The personal contact made the truths revealed in the Book of

Mormon mean even more to me than the reading, which I received in joy and gratitude.

I knew the Book of Mormon was a direct revelation from God in Christ by the ministry of the Spirit of truth. I rejoice that He has appointed a prophet to be among us and anointed a priesthood on our sorry planet. I am now studying the Doctrine and Covenants, still in amazement that our Lord has granted me knowledge beyond my highest expectations and friends in the truest sense.

IT RESTORES TRUTHS ABOUT CHRIST NOT FOUND IN THE BIBLE

TOM ROSS-BARNETT
Leeds, England

I was born in Liberia, West Africa, some thirty-seven years ago. The first nine years of my life were lived in abject poverty, as is the unfortunate norm for most of my countrymen. My life took a dramatic turn when I was brought to the United Kingdom in 1961 by an English lady who had been travelling through Africa on holiday. I was terribly crippled by poliomyelitis and was able to undergo medical treatment which greatly improved my life. [This story is told in detail in *The Grasshopper Boy,* by June Johns (London: Epworth Press, 1967).] This marvelous lady later adopted me. Through her I got the chance of an education and vast opportunities in life which otherwise would have been dreams. I attended Iowa Wesleyan College between 1971 and 1975, graduating in biology. I have since qualified as a schoolteacher and am working at the moment with people with learning disabilities.

I was baptized into The Church of Jesus Christ of Latter-day Saints in November 1980. I am grateful for my membership in Christ's only true church on the earth today. I am grateful for the opportunities I have had to grow in the scriptures and in the various callings I have held. I have been honored to serve as ward clerk, Sunday School president, Sunday School teacher, and institute teacher, as well as in the elders' quorum presidency, on the activities committee, and at the moment as first counselor in the bishopric of my ward, Gaerwen Ward, Chester England Stake.

I first came into contact with the Book of Mormon in the summer of 1973. While I was in the United States as a college student I visited Salt Lake City. In Temple Square I bought a copy of the Book of Mormon along with other souvenirs. I placed no significance on this because I knew nothing at all about the Church.

When the friends I was travelling with saw me with the Book of Mormon, they began to laugh and told me that I did not want to read "that book," as it represented a racist church. I found it strange that a church should be racist. Unfortunately, I did nothing to investigate for myself. But I kept the Book of Mormon, and it travelled around with me for the next seven years, though I never had the courage to read it — to France, to the U.K., back to the U.S., to West Africa and back to the U.K. again. Finally, in August 1980, when I was living in Leeds, England, I was stopped in the street by two missionaries. I took this opportunity to invite them home, with the intention of challenging them on all the negative stories I had heard about the Church.

Well, they did turn up and I did challenge them, and they did answer my questions. It was not their answers which impressed me the most, however. It was the challenge they left me with to read and find out for myself if what they had told me was true.

I am pleased to say that I have read, pondered, and prayed about these things. I have followed the entreaties of Moroni 10:3–5. I have put this to the test, and every question that bothered me about the Book of Mormon I have resolved through sincere desire, prayer, and studying. I have no hesitation in attesting to the truthfulness of the Book of Mormon. The Holy Ghost has shown me its authenticity. No other book makes Christ its central character as does the Book of Mormon. I testify that the Book of Mormon not only testifies of Jesus Christ but also restores some truths of Him not found in the Bible. Not only does it confirm the doctrines we learn about Christ in the Bible but it also adds to and amplifies them. I believe the Book of Mormon was written for us today. If only we would follow its precepts, our lives would be so much richer.

I AWAKENED MY WIFE AND TOLD HER OF MY DREAM

MUTOMBO K. ANTOINE
Kinshasa, Zaire

The first time I met the missionaries, in 1986, I immediately arranged for a meeting. After the first lesson, they offered me a copy of the Book of Mormon. It was strange to find another testament of Jesus Christ. I wondered what this meant, and my heart was troubled. The missionaries told me that by reading this book I could know whether or not it was true and that God, by the power of the Holy Ghost, would show me the truth of all things, as Moroni had said (Moroni 10:3–5) and as James has said (James 1:5). Following the example of the Prophet Joseph Smith, who asked wisdom of God, and putting into practice the recommendation of Moroni to know whether this book was true, I was shown a great truth — a most significant vision:

As I slept I dreamed that I was discussing with some other brethren the truths of this church. At the same time the Spirit of God led me to look to the sky, where I saw a golden globe. At one side, seated in a chair, was the Prophet Joseph Smith holding a copy of the Book of Mormon in his hands. Beyond that I saw the two thousand young soldiers of whom Helaman spoke. Behind all this stood the most beautiful building that I had ever seen — exactly like the picture of the temple in Salt

Lake City. What a wonderful thing! I quickly got up and awakened my wife and told her of my dream. Together we praised God. And from that time I have known that The Church of Jesus Christ of Latter-day Saints is the only true church on the earth, and that the Book of Mormon is a sacred book, a true testimony of Jesus Christ. And I know with all my heart that I am on the straight and narrow way of the Lord.

Everyone can, in this way, discover this wonderful truth by the power of the Holy Ghost.

I know that God lives, that Jesus Christ is the Son of God, that Joseph Smith was a prophet of God, and that Ezra Taft Benson is the living prophet on the earth who leads us in these latter days. He recommends that we read the Book of Mormon regularly. It is the keystone of our religion, and I love to follow this counsel. (Translated by Edwin Adamson.)

I HAD KNOWN JESUS WAS THE CHRIST, BUT IT TOLD ME WHY

ALBERTO MARRERO, JR.
Los Angeles, California

In April 1986 two missionaries stopped by and left a tract titled *Christ in America*. It was left with my daughter Miriam, and I read it only as a curiosity. What first struck me was the Mormon sense of God's universality. I then pursued the concept with a close friend of mine at work who was a Latter-day Saint. My LDS friend told me about the First Vision. I remember how I chuckled at the golden plates and gave it not another thought.

At this time, the only thing I knew about Mormons was that they were a peculiar people. I was aware of polygamy, and I thought that members of minority groups could not be Mormon church members. I also was under the impression that Mormons were radical "born-again, fundamentalist Christians."

A week later my LDS partner at work gave me a copy of *A Marvelous Work and a Wonder*. I read it more as a study than as a spiritual message. As I read that book, some of the questions that had for so long bothered me started to be answered.

After having finished *A Marvelous Work,* I asked my LDS friend for a copy of the Book of Mormon. I remember coming home, sitting poolside with a kahluá and milk in hand and reading the Book of Mormon. As I read, a struggle began to develop. Being well versed in history, I had serious doubts about the Book of Mormon societies in ancient America. But as I read on, my heart and my spirit became more and more involved in the Book of Mormon. Spiritual questions that had cursed me for years were being answered.

Every day my heart and soul were satisfied, quenched by the reading of the Book of Mormon. And every day at the end of each reading, my mind would say, "Yeah, but what about this? What about that?" As if by magic, the previous day's questions were answered during the next day's reading. I found myself being unable to keep away from the Book of Mormon.

By the time I had finished Alma, my heart and soul were convinced that this indeed was the word of God, but intellectually I still rejected the historicity of the Book of Mormon. As I pressed onward, I came to realize that philosophically, spiritually, I had always been a Mormon. I described my struggle to my LDS friend. He suggested prayer. I conscientiously refused to pray. I was afraid that I might fool myself, because I wanted a positive answer. I wanted hard, cold reality to go along with my spiritual understanding.

I woke up one Sunday morning in June 1986, and reality, knowledge, and faith all came together. I remember saying to myself, "You *know* that this is the word of God. You *know* that the Book of Mormon has moved you like no other book ever has. You *know* that this Book of Mormon is more real than the ground you are standing on." By denying the reality of the Book of Mormon, I was denying the most concrete reality I had ever experienced in my life.

Faith had become knowledge. For the first time in my life my spirit and my mind were in complete harmony. I went on to take the mandatory missionary lessons, but the Book of Mormon had already decided the issue.

I was baptized in August 1986, and since then my family has followed. I had always known that Jesus was the Christ, but it took the Book of Mormon to tell me why.

THE VOICE SAID, "I AM NOW GOING TO ANSWER YOUR PRAYERS"

RAJ KUMAR
Chandigarh, India

I was born in a very strong Hindu-Sikh family in Punjab, India, and in my adult life sought to know the truth about religion. I became a Christian but continued to feel unsatisfied and to pray for understanding. When I was pursuing a master's degree in Chandigarh in 1982, I went to a performance of the Young Ambassadors from Brigham Young University. Afterwards, while I was meeting some of the young people, the Spirit whispered to me to go back to my seat. I obeyed and then I heard a voice say clearly, "The time has come when I am going to answer your prayers. Go out and you will find a special young man. You will know him, and he will answer your questions." This touched me deeply and I again obeyed.

A young man named Thomas Nelson had just come out of the dressing room. As I met him I knew he was the special one, and I said to him, "You all seem to be strong Christians by nature. Why don't you announce that to your audiences and share the gospel directly?"

With great power and authority, he said to me, "We are Christians, but we are quite different from other Christians."

I said, "I am a Methodist. How are you different from me?"

Without hesitating, he asked me three questions, one after the other: "Have you ever heard about The Church of Jesus Christ of Latter-day Saints?"

"Have you ever heard about a book called the Book of Mormon?"

"Have you ever heard about a prophet called Joseph Smith?"

After each of these three questions, I felt a great sensation in my body, and I could almost feel the Holy Ghost talking to me as if He was bringing something to my remembrance. I could feel without any doubt that I was always familiar with these things, but at that time I felt that I had lost my memory and I was unable to explain what these things were.

I requested Brother Nelson to tell me more about the Church of Jesus Christ, the Book of Mormon, and the Prophet Joseph Smith. This good brother was very kind to me. He told me the sweetest story of the restoration of the gospel of Jesus Christ. It took him about thirty minutes to tell me this great story. Thirty minutes before, I did not know a thing about the Church, the Book of Mormon, or the Prophet Joseph Smith, but thirty minutes after, I knew without a shadow of doubt, as much as I know today, that The Church of Jesus Christ of Latter-day Saints is the only true church upon the face of this earth and the Book of Mormon is true and is the word of God. I also knew without any doubt that the man Joseph Smith was truly a prophet of God, a man who was instrumental in the hands of God in bringing about the restoration of the blessed gospel of Christ.

I expressed a desire to have a copy of the Book of Mormon. Brother Nelson did not have the book but promised me that he would send one to me soon. A few days later, I received a copy of the Book of Mormon through the mail. It is perhaps the greatest possession and gift I have ever received. This holy book is a great treasure, and I have received many wonderful and glorious blessings as I have made its study a habit. The Book of Mormon is a blessing in my life. I love this holy book and I would exhort all the inhabitants of this earth to read, study, ponder, and pray about this holy book. As much as I live, I promise that this book will prove a boon in the lives of its readers. I've come closer to the Lord my God as a result of regular study of the Book of Mormon. The Lord has taught me many great things as I've studied this holy book.

I would like to relate a very special experience that I had while I was serving as a full-time missionary in December 1983. I had just been transferred to the Fresno California Second Ward. I had been out only three months. I was a little discouraged and homesick. I wanted to serve the Lord and do my very best, but I was not able to get over this discouragement. I decided to seek help from the Lord through a regular study of the Book of Mormon. One morning I was reading this holy book in Alma 36:3, which reads, "For I do know that whosoever shall put their trust in God shall be supported in their trials, and their troubles, and their afflictions, and shall be lifted up at the last day." It could be just another verse in the book for many, but for me it has proved a great blessing. I could almost feel the prophet Alma standing in front of me that morning and talking to me. I was strengthened, and I started putting more faith in the direction and purpose in my life as a result of this. I study this holy book as often as possible, and the Lord continues to be my strength. I love the Book of Mormon, and I'm very thankful to the holy prophets who so faithfully wrote in this book the revelations and inspirations they received from our Heavenly Father.

My Guilt Was Burned and Washed Away

David Dollahite
Fairfax, California

I was raised in the Episcopal church in Fairfax, California. Though the traditional confirmation age in the Episcopal church is twelve, I was confirmed at age ten because I wanted to serve as an altar boy and because my parents were involved in lay positions in the church. I served as an altar boy for about two years.

When I was twelve I started playing Little League baseball, and because the games were on Sunday, I no longer wanted to attend church nor serve as an altar boy, and so stopped attending. My religion was sports from age twelve until about age nineteen, when I read the Book of Mormon. My life's goal was to play professional sports. I played baseball, basketball, and tennis, until I dropped other sports to concentrate on tennis at about age fifteen.

I played tennis about six hours a day, year round, from age fifteen almost to nineteen. I traveled throughout northern California playing tournaments, played on my high school team, and taught tennis in the summers. I attained a measure of success by winning several tournaments, playing number one singles, and being selected most valuable player on my high school's tennis team. I planned to play professional tennis and be a teaching pro at a large tennis club. I had no interest in school other than sports programs and friends, and no interest in books other than those that might help me play better tennis.

When I was seventeen and a junior in high school, I began to develop staph infections and bone bruises in both feet. Tests indicated that I would continue to have the foot problems if I continued playing tennis for many hours a day.

The injuries to my feet forced me to stay out of some important tournaments in my senior year of high school, and I lost some important matches that I needed to win to obtain tennis scholarships. So after high school graduation I stayed at home and attended a junior college, taking classes and not playing tennis.

The Book of Mormon arrived in our house through the efforts of Ray and LoDonna Leininger, friends of my parents. LoDonna worked with my mom and had told her much about The Church of Jesus Christ of Latter-day Saints and invited her to some church activities. My parents discussed the beliefs and practices of the Mormons around the dinner table on occasion and attended a few activities. They appeared fairly interested and complimentary. I began to think that my parents were going to become Mormons and told them to keep the Mormon religion away from me — I didn't want anything to do with it.

One day when I came home, I saw on the dining room table a blue paperback book with a picture of someone playing a trumpet — the Book of Mormon. To me, having the "Mormon Bible" in the house was more evidence that my parents were interested in joining the Church, but they said they were only politely listening because the Leiningers were friends of theirs. This turned out to be true. My mom put the book on the shelf, I forgot about it, and they stopped talking about the Mormons.

A couple of months later, in November 1977, I was at the end of my first semester of junior college and still didn't know what I wanted to do with life. I was quite discouraged that my prospects for playing tennis professionally seemed dashed. I was sitting at home alone absently watching television and a strange thought came into my mind — I should read a book! I reasoned that now that I was in college and wasn't going to be an athlete, I should probably do something academic. So I went over to the wall of bookshelves in our living room. I saw novels, histories, and autobiographies that looked interesting. (My mom was an avid reader, collecting hundreds of books, and it was usually my job to dust them.) But then my eye caught a little blue book in the extreme upper left-hand corner. Something told me to take that very book down and read it. I pulled it down and opened up the Book of Mormon. I didn't know why, but I sat down and started to read. I read about twenty pages and felt warm and cool at the same time. I felt a kind of warm tingling all over and thought that a window must be open, but I checked and they were all closed. I began feeling that there was something very important about this book, that there were things being taught in this book that would be important for me to learn and understand.

I had to go to work that evening at a movie theater, so I put the book down. I thought about religion during my drive to work, about the things that were talked about in the Book of Mormon, about this family of Lehi who believed so strongly in their God that they were willing to leave their home and go through many difficulties.

As the movie played, I took my turn behind the concession stand, still thinking about religion, thinking that perhaps I ought to find out more about religion, that maybe religion would be helpful to me. A strange, disheveled man came out of the theater and walked up to me, pulled a pack of cigarettes out of his pocket, and said, "These are Camel cigarettes. I used to smoke Cool cigarettes, but God came to me in a vision and told me that I should smoke Camel cigarettes." He told me about how God had spoken to him and told him to do various strange things. I thought that if this is what religion was all about, I didn't want anything to do with it.

I also remembered that a couple of months before, my best friend and doubles partner had gone off to New York, had been mugged, and was rescued and converted by a born-again minister. My friend called me from New York and told me that I was a sinner and needed to repent and accept Jesus or I would go to hell. He sounded strange and seemed so rigid and judgmental. I began again to feel my normal reaction that religion was not for me and that I shouldn't waste my time reading the Book of Mormon.

But when I got home from work that night about 9:30, I again had a powerful feeling urging me to read the Book of Mormon. I went downstairs, got the book, brought it up to my room, sat down, and began to read. Again I felt those strange warm chills I had never felt before. I admired Nephi. He seemed to be a strong and courageous person. I also admired the prophet Abinadi, who was willing to suffer torture and death because of his belief in God. These prophets were not the weak men I'd assumed religion would make them. I felt anticipation as I read about the coming visit of Jesus Christ to the people in the Book of Mormon. Although I had heard about Jesus Christ, I had never read the Bible nor really cared one way or another about who Christ was or why I should know His teachings.

I read through the night until about 6 A.M. Many times I wanted to stop. I couldn't understand why I was sitting up all night reading any book, much less a religious book. There wasn't reason in that. I thought that if my friends could see me staying up all night reading a book about Jesus they would really give me a hard time. I was tired and sore and wanted to sleep, but I couldn't put the book down. Though the strong feelings were strange, they felt wonderful.

I went to school that day and to work that night and thought deeply about the things I had read. Something was happening within me. I began to feel sorrow for my sins and began to desire to be different, to be more like the people I was reading about. I had a strong desire to read the Book of Mormon, more than to do anything else. I rushed home from work that night and sat down at the same desk in my room and began to read. Again I read though the night. Many times I wanted to stop because of fatigue and hunger, but I sensed that there was something waiting for me at the end of the book that I needed to read. So I read on.

When I came to where Jesus Christ visited the people of America and read what He did and taught, I was on the verge of tears. I read with great joy the words that Jesus spoke to the people, and I knew that what He was saying was true. His actions and words touched something deep within me. I loved Jesus and wanted to be with Him. I felt sorrow for my sins, and I knew that I needed forgiveness. Somehow I knew that He was the Son of God and that it was very important for me to learn about Him and to have Him become a part of my life.

When I got about ten pages from the end of the book and could see that I was nearly finished, it was about 5 A.M. after the second night. I was weary and wanted very much to sleep. My eyes and back were tired and sore. I thought, I'll just read the rest of this tomorrow. But then another strong feeling compelled me to continue reading to the end.

I suddenly felt wide awake, as if I had awoken from a ten-hour sleep. I got to Moroni 10:3–5, which were marked with lines and the phrase "very important verses." I read these verses several times, finally understanding what these verses were asking me to do. I thought about how merciful the Lord had been to humanity and to me. I pondered the things that I had read, the teachings about Jesus, the purpose of life, the great sacrifices that people were willing to make for their belief in God, the teachings of Christ, and I thought about the feelings I had as I read. I didn't understand what they were. I didn't know where those feelings came from. I just knew that I had never felt that way before. And I thought about my sins. I also sensed deep within that there was something extremely important about this book.

Then I realized that the verses were also asking me to ask God in prayer if what I had read was true. I had never prayed before, though I had said the Lord's Prayer in church many times and had read other prayers in the Book of Common Prayer. But I had never prayed to God "with a sincere heart, with real intent, having faith in Christ." I knew that this was what I needed to do.

I knelt in my room and prayed that God would forgive me of my sins and tell me if the things that I had read in the Book of Mormon were true. During that prayer, I had a profound spiritual experience. I felt an intense and overwhelming magnification of the feelings that I had felt all the way through the Book of Mormon. I felt as if my body were on fire and at the same time as if waves of water were pouring over and through me. My guilt was burned and washed away. I felt almost as if I were lifted off the ground or lifted out of my body. New knowledge flowed into my mind, and new feelings poured into my heart. The truthfulness of the Book of Mormon was burned into my soul. I felt completely at one with God and with all people. I no longer desired to follow *my* goals or *my* desires but only wanted to be close to God and all people.

Many small pictures flowed through my mind, small

glimpses of what seemed to be my future: pictures and feelings of me living a righteous life and teaching others about Jesus Christ and the Book of Mormon, and many other scenes I didn't understand. I had glimpses of a profound connection with all people, and of relationships with the prophets I had read about, of spending time with great souls learning about the wonders of the universe. I know that this was God's answer to my prayer. I wept for a long time at the joy of knowing that God knew about me and loved me, that my life was not an accident, of knowing that I had been taken off a path that could have led to destruction and being placed on a path that would lead to joy and peace. My prayer and experience must have lasted close to thirty minutes. Everything changed in that prayer—my thoughts, feelings, desires, and longings. I felt like my mind and heart and spirit were completely cleansed and that I was like a container, waiting to be filled.

When I arose from my knees, went to my bed and lay down, I couldn't sleep. Thoughts were rushing through my mind that this was the most important day of my life, that everything from this day on would be different. I knew more than I had ever known anything in my life that there was a God, that Jesus Christ was the Son of God, that I had been forgiven of my sins because of what he did, and that the Book of Mormon was God's word. I asked my mom at breakfast to tell Sister Leininger that I had read the Book of Mormon and wanted to know more about the Church. She invited me to church that Sunday, and I had my first missionary lesson that Sunday night. I felt the same feelings in church and during the missionary lessons that I had had while reading the Book of Mormon. One of the elders in that first discussion identified the feeling as coming from the Holy Ghost. I did not doubt thereafter and was baptized about a month later on January 28, 1978.

The Lord knew that I would probably not have listened to any person who tried to convert me to a religion and instead compelled me to read on my own and blessed me with an outpouring of his Spirit. I have never doubted since that morning that God answers sincere prayer and that the Book of Mormon is the word of God. Because of my experience, I wanted to tell everyone I knew and met about the Book of Mormon and Jesus Christ. I have had the blessing of teaching many about the Book of Mormon and seeing it lead them to Christ. Through the years that I have been a member of the Church, the Book of Mormon has been a constant source of faith and strength and truth to me. I have read it more than any other book. I have studied its pages, thought about its doctrines, tried to live its precepts, and received great blessings as a result. I now keep a copy of the Book of Mormon in the upper left-hand corner of my bookshelf to remind me of what is important and where all my blessings come from.

RECONVERSIONS

Here are testimonies from thirteen people who were baptized as children and raised in the Church but only came to know the Book of Mormon was true—or to appreciate it in new and more complete ways—later in their lives. They range from persons who were given sudden dramatic experiences, much like those of new converts, to some who gradually came to joyous conviction and understanding after long study, to some who had both; from those who seem somewhat afflicted by testimonies they can't escape to those who have found essential comfort to go on living; from those who find insights into their sins and into Christ's atonement to those who find a new sense of their own identity—as a Polynesian "Lamanite," as a musician, as a father. And for some, there is an inescapable discovery of beauty.

THE EXPERIENCE WAS FOR ME, NOT SO MUCH FOR HER

WILLIAM A. WILSON
Jyväskylä, Finland

It was a decrepit part of town, an old part of town by the ski jump. Winding, meandering roads ran through the area. They weren't straight streets. The frame houses were small and separated from each other. It was probably one of the oldest parts of Jyväskylä, Finland. There we found a little old lady, a *mummo,* who lived in a little shack that has since been torn down. (The last time I returned there, it had been replaced with a new apartment building.) I don't think the old lady ever really understood much of what we were talking about, because she seemed more concerned that we were out there in the cold winter. We went out there dressed like Mormon missionaries always do, in light top coats. The *mummo* had enough clothing on and was all bundled up running around in that little old house that was never very warm. She probably had ten pairs of stockings on and many kinds of woolen underwear and so forth.

She always worried about us when we went there, worried that we were going to freeze to death. She kept inviting us back, so we kept going for a while, and then we just gave up when we could see that there was nothing at all coming from it. And that, I guess, is why the experience with the Book of Mormon meant more to me than if the woman had actually been converted, because I felt that the experience was for me, not so much for her.

In the missionary plan in those days, after you had told the story, you were supposed to testify to the validity of the Book of Mormon, and missionaries usually did that, sometimes sincerely, sometimes because it was in the plan. In the past I had been reasonably honest when I gave that testimony. But, as a general conference speaker said, there's a difference between a testimony, which is knowledge, and faith, which is believing. I think that I had the belief but not the testimony of the Book of Mormon. But that particular day, after we gave the Book of Mormon lesson, I was sitting there in the chair with my arm outstretched, the Book of Mormon lying open in my hand. As I said the words that testified to the truthfulness of the Book of Mormon, I felt a kind of an impulse, or a feeling as though some kind of electrical current was sweeping up my arm from the Book of Mormon into the rest of me. It felt as if the arm was transmitting some kind of vibration from the book to me. Anyway, that's the way I recall it after all these years. I can't remember all of it or the exact sensation; it has been too many years. I don't know if at that particular moment I felt that I had just had a witness to the Book of Mormon. I must have felt something because, as I say, I still remember the experience enough to talk about it, but the details slip away. It seems to me there was that sensation of the electrical, fiery feeling shooting up my arm from the book.

Whether there was an immediate effect on me of strong spiritual experience — the recognition of one — I don't remember, but after that I gave better Book of Mormon lessons, and from that time on the Book of Mormon has been the mainstay of my testimony. The Book of Mormon is very important to me because it, more than anything else, has helped me through difficult times when I have doubted other things and questioned other things. I have never been able to explain away the Book of Mormon. And if the Book of Mormon is true, then other things about the Church have to be true as well. If the Book of Mormon is not true, then you can explain away Joseph Smith's vision and his account; but if it is true, then you pretty much have to accept what he tells about it. There are things I don't understand, for example, polygamy and the Negro issue, but I'm not willing to give up the Church because of those things, mainly because of the conviction that goes back to the Book of Mormon and suggests to me that in these areas I don't understand I have to be tolerant and wait until I do.

The experience I had in Jyväskylä that cold day in 1956 was a witness I can't deny. I don't need films or "scientific" books to base my testimony on, because the promise Moroni made at the end of the book has in my case been fulfilled. The evidence of books and films may easily fail, but the evidence of a personal witness will endure. (From a tape-recorded interview.)

I Gained New Light on Christ's Relationship to Our Sins

Lowell Bennion
Seattle, Washington

In the summer of 1936 I went to summer school at the Uni-

versity of Washington. My purpose in going there was to take
courses in the archaeology of the western hemisphere. I had
recently been appointed a teacher at the institute of religion
near the University of Utah. One of the courses I offered was
on the Book of Mormon. I went to the University of Washington
in search of external evidence for the authenticity of the Book
of Mormon.

I studied hard, took copious notes, and listened eagerly to
my professors. I made a list of all the things in archaeology
that I might be able to relate to the Book of Mormon.

When the course was over, I hid out and read the Book
of Mormon with my archaeological notes before me. To my
surprise, I found few things I could relate to archaeological
data. I learned also that a person has to be an archaeologist
to be able to use scientific data judiciously.

Reading the book and analyzing its content gave me another
surprise. I discovered for the first time, and very forcefully,
that the Book of Mormon is not a scientific work, not history,
not a geographical treatise, not a theology text, but a profoundly
religious record, relating religion to life. It so declares its
purpose:

"And it mattereth not to me that I am particular to give a
full account of all the things of my father, for they cannot be
written upon these plates, for I desire the room that I may
write of the things of God.

"For the fulness of mine intent is that I may persuade men
to come unto the God of Abraham, and the God of Isaac, and
the God of Jacob, and be saved." (1 Nephi 6:3–4.)

Ever since 1936, my interest in reading and teaching the
Book of Mormon has been to look for its religious teaching
and spirit, and I have found the search rewarding. Permit a
few illustrations.

I performed the marriage ceremony for a young Mormon
woman and a young Jewish man who was a convert to Chris-
tianity. In a casual conversation, he asked, "Since we have the
New Testament, what does the Book of Mormon add to our

Christian faith?" That's a good question. Part of my answer is that the Book of Mormon greatly enriches our understanding of the first principles and ordinances of the gospel by which we become disciples of Christ:

1. Alma 32 is the finest statement on faith in all of scripture.

2. Repentance is the dominant theme of the Book of Mormon, beautifully expressed in Alma 5 and 7.

3. The meaning of baptism is stated explicitly in Mosiah 18:8–14.

4. The relationship of the Holy Ghost to the Christian virtues of humility and love is detailed in Moroni 8:24–26.

5. The meaning of the sacrament is spelled out with simplicity and rich meaning in the sacramental prayers. (See Moroni 4 and 5.)

The Book of Mormon is Christ-centered, bearing repeated witness of His mission. It has made some original and inspiring contributions to my understanding of the Atonement and of Christ's relationship to us.

When Jesus went to John the Baptist to be baptized, John hesitated, saying, "I have need to be baptized of thee, and comest thou to me?" (Matthew 3:14.) Jesus replied, "Suffer it to be so now: for thus it becometh us to fulfil all righteousness." (V. 15.) What He meant by that statement is not explained in the New Testament. But Nephi gives an inspiring interpretation:

"Know ye not that he was holy? But notwithstanding he being holy, he showeth unto the children of men that, according to the flesh he humbleth himself before the Father, and witnesseth unto the Father that he would be obedient unto him in keeping his commandments." (2 Nephi 31:7.)

It is inspiring to me to know that Jesus wanted to be baptized for His own sake, to show the Father that He would fulfill all righteousness by doing the Father's will.

The Book of Mormon throws light on Christ's relationship to the sins of men. King Benjamin, in his fine farewell sermon, says:

"And lo, he [Jesus] shall suffer temptations, and pain of

body, hunger, thirst, and fatigue, even more than man can suffer, except it be unto death; for behold, blood cometh from every pore, *so great shall be his anguish for the wickedness and the abominations of his people."* (Mosiah 3:7; italics added.)

Jesus loves His fellowmen so much that the fact that they are steeped in sin causes Him to suffer because they are ruining their lives in sin.

In his great sermon on the Atonement and repentance Amulek gives us a profound idea of Christ's relationship to our sins:

"And behold, this is the whole meaning of the law, every whit pointing to that great and last sacrifice; and that great and last sacrifice will be the Son of God, yea, infinite and eternal.

"And thus he shall bring salvation to all those who shall believe on his name; this being the intent of this last sacrifice, to bring about the bowels of mercy, which overpowereth justice, *and bringeth about means unto men that they may have faith unto repentance.*

"And thus mercy can satisfy the demands of justice, and encircles them in the arms of safety, while he that exercises no faith unto repentance is exposed to the whole law of the demands of justice; therefore only unto him that has faith unto repentance is brought about the great and eternal plan of redemption." (Alma 34:14–16; italics added.)

The only way to overcome sin is by repentance. Believing in and loving the Savior and doing His will gives people the faith, the motivation, to repent and thus be whole and be forgiven. Repentance enables mercy to satisfy the demands of justice. The Book of Mormon brings Christ into our lives in very meaningful ways.

When I was a missionary, a brother came to me broken-hearted because of a serious sin he had committed. With the Psalmist, he cried, "Create in me a clean heart, O God; and renew a right spirit within me." (Psalm 51:10.) At the close of our conversation, I invited him to prepare the sacrament table each Sunday morning. This he did reverently and lovingly.

After a few weeks, he came to me again and said, "I am a new man." He taught me that I too could find faith unto repentance in fellowship with the Savior.

I wish to mention one other idea that bears witness to me of the authenticity of the Book of Mormon. Many of its finest teachings grow out of natural settings. For example, Alma the Younger went on a preaching tour, going from settlement to settlement among his Nephite people. He found a group of people who had been cast out of their synagogue because of their exceeding poverty.

Alma said to them: "It is well that ye are cast out of your synagogues, that ye may be humble, and that ye may learn wisdom; for it is necessary that ye should learn wisdom; for it is because that ye are cast out, that ye are despised of your brethren because of your exceeding poverty, that ye are brought to a lowliness of heart; for ye are necessarily brought to be humble.

"And now, because ye are compelled to be humble blessed are ye; for a man *sometimes,* if he is compelled to be humble, seeketh repentance; and now surely, whosoever repenteth shall find mercy; and he that findeth mercy and endureth to the end the same shall be saved." (Alma 32:12–13; italics added.)

He wisely stated that external circumstances sometimes compelled a person to be humble. That is true to life, because externally compelled humbleness can cause people sometimes to be bitter and cynical, whereas a person who is humble because of the word of God enjoys true humility.

As a missionary in Germany I was reading one evening Alma 62:41, which states:

"But behold, because of the exceedingly great length of the war between the Nephites and the Lamanites many had become hardened, because of the exceedingly great length of the war; and many were softened because of their afflictions, insomuch that they did humble themselves before God, even in the depth of humility."

I thought, how true to life. As we tracted from door to door

a few years after Germany's defeat in World War I and saw the
people's suffering, we found many Germans bitter and asking
how God could permit such suffering. And we met many who
were humble and compassionate as a result of their suffering.
Ever since, I have observed how suffering and privation affect
people. I find it either hardens or refines them, just as the
Book of Mormon observed in that day.

I find that the Book of Mormon is an honest, true-to-life
reporting of human experience, and I am particularly grateful
for its insights concerning our relationship to Jesus Christ.

WITHOUT THE SPECTACULAR WITNESS, STILL IT BLESSES ME

MERRILL BRADSHAW
Provo, Utah

I have never had any reason to question those who talk of
miraculous manifestations about the Book of Mormon. Those
things have just never happened to me. In my younger years
I used to wonder if there were something wrong with me,
because when I prayed about the book nothing happened. I
suppose the real reason nothing ever happened is that I have
always had faith in the Book of Mormon and simply felt that
when I understood all there was to understand about it, all
the questions that other people raise about it would be answered and the book would still stand.

As a result, I cannot say, as so many are able to do, that
when I arose from praying about the book I had a burning
feeling that said, "That book is true." I have to think there are
a lot of us in the Church who are in a situation similar to mine.
But what I would like to emphasize here is that even without
the flashing lights or secret voices to tell me the Book of Mormon
is true, I have spent a good deal of time through my life studying
it and its coming forth and the various evidences that exist. I
cannot claim to have thought through all the questions that

disturb so many people, but I have a simple understanding that when we know everything there is to know about the book, it will still stand fast as the anchor to our faith that it has always been for me. Even without the spectacular witness, it still blesses me and my family greatly. Let me give some examples.

When I went on my mission to Switzerland in 1950, I had studied the German language in both high school and college for a total of three years. I thought I was well prepared to be a missionary, even though I had not read the Book of Mormon in its entirety. But in the encounter with the living language of the Swiss people and their dialects, I was overwhelmed. It became very difficult to apply what I had learned. My companion and I read aloud to each other for an hour each morning from the Max Zimmer German translation of the Book of Mormon, which was written in the old German script. It was tough going at first, but through that reading of the Book of Mormon in German, the rhythm and flow of the language became a reality for me, and I was soon able to use my training to good effect.

That early-morning reading also helped me get through the Isaiah chapters of 2 Nephi, which stymie so many, especially young readers. In the process I was introduced to the intriguing and beautiful poetry of Isaiah, to the vision he had of the whole history of man, to his strong concern for the poor and the widows. That began a life-long study of the whole book of Isaiah, which has been a blessing at many times of spiritual need or of spiritual high points.

That reading also opened up to me the way prophets have of placing things of our life here and now into a perspective that gives them their true meaning in eternity. These openings and beginnings have continued to enrich my understanding of the gospel, of the plan of salvation, of my values and goals, of the meaning of my own life. This all began with that hour we spent together reading the Book of Mormon to each other in the early mornings in an attic room in Bern, Switzerland. It was not just the language, but also the beginnings of an understanding of the beauty and importance of all scripture that came to me through that experience.

During a spring term at Brigham Young University a few years ago, I had the privilege of attending a seminar intended to train faculty to teach Book of Mormon classes for freshmen. During that six-week period I read the book through twice, outlining and pondering meanings as I went, savoring especially beautiful passages and doctrines. That marked a step up in my love for the book. I was able to get much closer to it and to pursue subjects and themes that attracted my interest.

Again, I cannot say that I received any special manifestation or witness. That was not a part of my relation to the book. Rather, I gained a heightened awareness of the beauty of its message and the importance of its warnings for people living in our time. This awareness has increased during the past year as I have been teaching the Book of Mormon in our Gospel Doctrine class. I have come to identify with the problems that men like Alma and Mormon had and to understand their deep concerns for people like me. I have learned that many of the details that are objected to by critics of the book pale by comparison with the magnificent and intense love that Christ shows in the preservation of the book so that we could have it to help us.

As a family we have read the book often in our scripture sessions. I would not claim to be as regular at this as we are encouraged to be, but probably more than half of the time we have spent together reading the scriptures has been spent reading the Book of Mormon. We have enjoyed those times together very much, the older children often speaking with great nostalgia about them. As our five missionaries have gone out, they have been prepared about the same as I was: they accepted the book as true, even though they had not read all of it many times nor had someone from the other world appeared to demand that they accept it. Yet even without those excellent and spectacular spiritual experiences, it is an anchor to our family, to our faith, to our whole way of life. It is the keystone of our religion in that intimate sense that it is one of the determinants of our existence. When I think of its significance to us, I wonder if any manifestation could be more important than that.

The Holy Ghost is not always obvious nor direct in His workings with us. But through small things happening over a lifetime, He forges a rock at the foundations of our beings that we can build good and happy lives on, lives that are productive and solid in the kingdom. The Book of Mormon is part of that rock for me, and its significance continues to increase for me. I am grateful to God for its blessing.

I Felt Nephi Was Talking to Me As One of His Seed

Sipuao Matuauto
Salt Lake City, Utah

When I reached the age of four, in our little village in Samoa my mother taught me how to read, using the Samoan version of the Book of Mormon. I was a fast learner, and as I carefully followed Mother's reading and pronunciation guidelines, soon I was able to read the Book of Mormon and other scriptures by myself.

At the age of six, I completed reading the Book of Mormon entirely. Mother was extremely proud of my accomplishment and helped me set and accomplish the goal of reading the Bible, both the Old and New Testaments, by the age of seven.

At the age of twelve, I began reading the English version of the Book of Mormon in elementary school. Our missionary teachers also held Book of Mormon study classes in the evenings, which I was privileged to attend. As a young teenager I became more interested in reading the English versions of the scriptures— somehow, they made more sense to me than the Samoan versions.

Throughout my life, I have studied and read all the scriptures daily. Ever since I was a child, I have known of their truthfulness and have constantly expressed a deep appreciation to the Lord for these priceless records and the efforts of the great men and women who preserved these records for my benefit. I never felt the need of receiving a personal witness from the Spirit. I just knew they were true.

On Saturday, August 12, 1972, I came down with laryngitis. I had moved to Salt Lake City, Utah, and was a member of the Mormon Tabernacle Choir at the time, so I called Richard P. Condie, the director, and asked to be excused from the choir broadcast the next morning. He strongly advised me to stay home and take care of myself. He also discouraged me from talking throughout the duration of the weekend. After hanging up the telephone, I locked the door of my bedroom and immediately tried to determine what I could do to have a wonderful, profitable weekend, despite my dilemma. I was not ill, I had just lost my voice, and I felt I could still accomplish something worthwhile.

Of all the scriptures and many other great Church books available, I simply picked up a worn-out copy of the Book of Mormon and started reading it. This was nothing new to me, and I most certainly had not expected that anything out of the ordinary would happen to me; but somehow as I started reading it this time, I felt a powerful force that overwhelmed and overcame me at the same time, one which I had never before experienced in my many years of reading and studying this sacred record.

As I kept on reading I strangely and strongly felt that I belonged to the Book of Mormon people. I did my best to subdue these feelings, but the more I did, the deeper and closer I felt to them. Finally I came to the words of Nephi, prophesying the coming forth of the Book of Mormon:

"Wherefore, for this cause hath the Lord God promised unto me that these things which I write shall be kept and preserved, and handed down unto my seed, from generation to generation, that the promise may be fulfilled unto Joseph, that his seed should never perish as long as the earth should stand. . . .

"After my seed and the seed of my brethren shall have dwindled in unbelief, and shall have been smitten by the Gentiles; . . . and after they shall have been brought down low in the dust, even that they are not, yet the words of the righteous shall be written, and the prayers of the faithful shall be heard, and all those who have dwindled in unbelief shall not be forgotten. For those who shall be destroyed shall speak unto them out of the ground, and their speech shall be low out of the dust, and their voice shall be as one that hath a familiar spirit; for the Lord God will give unto him power, that he may whisper concerning them, even as it were out of the ground; and their speech shall whisper out of the dust." (2 Nephi 25:21; 26:15–16.)

The emotions that were building up within me could no longer be controlled. I burst into tears and cried for an hour or two. I felt as if Nephi of old was sitting there with me in my room, talking directly to me as if I were his seed; and my bosom swelled with a great abundance of love for this noble man, Nephi. I began to feel so very close to him and felt as if I had personally known him and lived during his time. As I dried my tears away, my heart was deeply touched by the efforts of this great prophet and others who had recorded and preserved these writings and instructions for their descendants and all those who would faithfully follow the Lord of the Book of Mormon, Jesus Christ.

As powerful as this experience was, however, a little confusion was beginning to form in my mind. You see, as a youngster, growing up in Samoa, I had always been told that we were Lamanite descendants, which was contrary to the feelings I was experiencing as I read the words of Nephi. I could not understand how I could possibly be of Nephi's seed if I was a descendant of Laman. I admit the thought startled me, and yet, almost immediately, the Spirit impressed me to turn to Alma

63 and read about Hagoth, the ship builder. As I read this chapter, I discovered the following:

"And it came to pass that Hagoth, he being an exceedingly curious man, therefore he went forth and built him an exceedingly large ship, on the borders of the land Bountiful, by the land Desolation, and launched it forth into the west sea, by the narrow neck which led into the land northward. And behold, there were many of the *Nephites* who did enter therein and did sail forth with much provisions, and also many women and children; and they took their course northward. And thus ended the thirty and seventh year.... And it came to pass that they were never heard of more. And we suppose that they were drowned in the depths of the sea. And it came to pass that one other ship also did sail forth; and whither she did go we know not." (Alma 63:5–6, 8; italics added.)

This gave me the answer I needed. I came to realize that it was very possible that the blood of both Nephi and Laman flows in my veins. The scripture is clear that the people who were on the two lost ships were Nephites; but at the time when Hagoth built his ships, both the righteous Nephites and the righteous Lamanites, who were members of the Church, were collectively identified as Nephites.

Long before Hagoth started building his ships, King Lamoni and his people and also his father and his people were converted to the gospel by Ammon and his brethren. They were faithful and devoted. There is no doubt in my mind that some of them were on these lost ships with their white brethren. It was also probable that the people who were on these lost ships eventually intermarried. I remembered, too, that thoughout the Book of Mormon many Nephites mixed with the unconverted Lamanites and they were collectively identified as Lamanites.

As I read this chapter under the influence of the Holy Spirit, I received a personal witness that the strong, deep feelings I was experiencing, and had tried to subdue, were justified.

This also explains a strange dream I had six months earlier.

The dream was very brief, but it startled me and woke me up right out of bed. In the dream, a tall, handsome gentleman dressed in a white robe was standing before me and introduced himself. He said, "I am Joseph who was sold into Egypt. I am your father." The effect of the dream woke me up, and I could not return to sleep for the rest of the night. In the days that followed I felt as if I were in another sphere. Also, a paragraph from my patriarchal blessing began to make more sense.

Now after I had read Alma 63, everything made sense to me. After I discovered this information, I knelt down on my knees and offered Heavenly Father a simple prayer of thanksgiving for helping me eliminate my confusion, the confusion that had been caused by something I was told as a youngster.

By Saturday midnight, I got to the chapters on the Savior's visit to the Americas. Here again, I had to stop for another hour. My emotions were too much to be subdued. I felt the sweet presence of the Savior in my room as if He, too, were sitting there with me, telling me to be faithful and keep His commandments. What a glorious experience! I felt with every fiber of my trembling body the power of every word proceeding from His mouth as He talked to the Nephites. Again, I got down on my knees and, at this time, made a commitment to the Savior that never, never in my life will I disappoint Him.

I never did sleep Saturday night—the power of this great sacred record was too overwhelming for me to stop, to say the least. I kept on reading, and by 8:00 Sunday night, my reading was ended and the book was quietly closed and was returned to the shelf; but the grandness and the sweetness of the overpowering Spirit I had experienced remained with me for some time.

Two weeks later I was in Mexico City, attending the Mexico and Central America Area Conference. The Mormon Tabernacle Choir was to provide the music for both conference sessions on Sunday. On Saturday afternoon we went to the building where the conference was held to rehearse. As the choir members walked on stage to be seated for the rehearsal, the Mexican sisters were leaving a women's meeting. As I approached the stairs to go up on stage to be seated, a group of those "Lamanite" sisters saw me and excitedly rushed over, speaking Spanish to me. I smiled at them and said hello. Although I could not communicate with them, somehow I felt one with them and understood what they were saying. They had mistakenly thought I was of Mexican descent and were excited to see that one of their own participated in the greatest choir on earth. I wished I could speak Spanish to return their excitement.

Fortunately, one of the sisters spoke English, and I explained to them through her that although I did not speak their language, I was still one of their own through our common ancestral father, Lehi. At this point the sisters huddled around and hugged me and kissed me.

During both sessions on Sunday, as I sat on stage I strongly felt the same feelings I had experienced two weekends earlier in my room in Salt Lake City as I was reading the Book of Mormon. Looking out to this vast audience of Lamanites, I felt at home with them. I felt as if I were looking at a Polynesian audience. The Spirit was powerful and I knew without a shadow of a doubt that Lehi, Nephi, and all the Book of Mormon prophets were in attendance. I sat there with tears streaming down my cheeks as the Spirit bore witness to my soul that these were truly my people. The blood of the same ancestral lineage runs through my veins and their veins. The local priesthood leaders who spoke at the conference were giants of men. I understood their feelings and what they were saying, even though I do not speak their language. In such a short time, I came to know and to love them just as much as I love the Polynesians. I felt as if I had finally met the relatives I had often heard about but had never met.

Through this experience, I came to realize the great love and mercy the Lord had for me. He had allowed me the opportunity to prepare myself for a glorious experience in Mexico City. I was impressed that Christ can be my personal friend and confidant as well as my Savior. Ever since then, as I continue to study the Book of Mormon daily, I have come to cherish and treasure it as the sacred record of my ancestors and my people. Their writings and their exemplary lives have greatly enriched mine. Through their efforts, I have come to know the Savior, Jesus Christ, as they knew Him.

It Seemed That Nephi Was There and Spoke to My Heart

George Pace
Burley, Idaho

The following account is from Our Search to Know the Lord, *by George Pace (Salt Lake City: Deseret Book, 1988), pages 8– 10. Reprinted by permission.*

I was raised as an active member of a small country ward in southern Idaho. I sensed early in my life that the testimonies I heard in the small frame chapel each fast and testimony meeting were sincere and indeed true. I felt very positive about the teachings I heard and the concepts I learned in the many auxiliary meetings I attended. I observed also that the more diligently I tried to keep the commandments and to stay in close contact with the Church, although I often fell far short, the more peace I felt in my heart. And even though much of the motivation behind my activity in the Church was probably social (there were some really attractive girls in the ward), my involvement in the Church was uplifting and beneficial.

Nevertheless, had I been asked in my late teens how I felt about the Church—that is, did I know the doctrines of the Church were true?—my response would have been something like, "I really think there is a strong possibility that the Church just might be true," or, "There is absolutely no question in my mind that a lot of people I know really know the Church is true," or, "Oh, I sure hope the Church is true!" In any event, even though I felt very good about the Church—indeed, there was absolutely no question in my mind that the effect of the Church in my life was very positive—I knew there had to be much, much more to my membership. I sensed that I hadn't yet found that pearl of great price that would give greater meaning to my membership in the Church and enable me to obtain a greater power to enjoy life more abundantly.

Somewhere along the line, I came to the conclusion that I desperately needed to learn more fully for myself by personal revelation that Joseph Smith was a prophet of God and that the true Church of Jesus Christ was indeed restored to the earth. I determined that the quickest, surest way to do that was to read the Book of Mormon and pray mightily about it. Consequently, in my nineteenth year [1950] and while farming my father's farm, I decided to tuck a copy of the Book of Mormon in my back pocket and take it with me everywhere I went. I carried out my plan with some determination. Whenever I got a chance between changes of water while irrigating, while waiting for the final preparation of my meals, and during every other spare moment I could find, I read the Book of Mormon with genuine intensity for the first time. I had, of course, read portions of it before, both in the auxiliaries and in seminary, but not really of my own volition and not with real intent. Along with diligently reading the Book of Mormon every time I got a chance, for the first time in my life, I also lifted up my voice many times each day in mighty vocal prayer and pleaded for the witness of the Spirit that I might know that the Book of Mormon is true.

My experience that summer of reading the Book of Mormon and fervently pouring out my heart in prayer changed my life. Before the summer was half over, it seemed I had walked into a whole new dimension of life. The unseen things of the Spirit started to become more real than the things of the world. There gradually deepened in my heart the unquestionable assurance that what I was reading was true, and with that revealed assurance, Joseph Smith's divine calling as a prophet of God emerged as my great anchor in the reality of the restoration of the gospel. With those assurances, there seemed to come to me a desire to be more personally involved in the great unfolding drama of the redemption of man, a feeling that there was a preparation to be made, a mission to be fulfilled, a reason for being. Incidentally, I've noticed over the years that when anyone obtains a sure testimony of the divine origins of the Church, invariably that person will get excited about doing all he or she can do to effectively build the kingdom.

As beautiful and as great as those feelings were, however, I still hadn't glimpsed what the real pearl was. One experience I had that summer made a particularly deep impression on me and seemed to bring me a step closer to finding the pearl of greatest price. I had been irrigating alfalfa, a task that gave me several hours for reading interspersed with vocal prayer. About midmorning, I was sitting on a small bridge made of railroad ties that crossed the irrigation ditch. I was dangling my rubber boots in the water to keep my feet cool. As I sat there reading and reflecting, there came to me a quiet but particularly powerful witness of the Spirit that what I was reading was true. The feeling was so intense that I instinctively glanced heavenward. Although I didn't see anyone or hear anything, I seemed to feel strongly the presence of Nephi— so strongly, in fact, that I wouldn't have been at all surprised to have seen him standing there. It seemed to me that he spoke to my heart and said: "I want you to know that what you're reading is true, for I wrote it. I want you to know that I have seen the Lord and talked with him. I have been carried by his Spirit to the tops of high mountains and have been shown marvelous things. [See 2 Nephi 4:24–25.] And I want you to know he has endowed me with great power to fulfill all the commandments he has given me."

What a great assurance it was for me to feel so deeply and powerfully the truth of Nephi's words, and especially to know of his relationship with the Lord and of the great power the Lord had given him. As the summer continued and I persisted in reading and lifting up my voice in prayer, there came into my heart, by the power of the Spirit, an even greater and more exciting idea, an idea that helped me learn more fully what the gospel was really all about. It seemed to come from the Spirit and reflected the testimony of Nephi. The message was: "It's wonderful that you now know that what I have written is true, and that you know I have seen and talked with Christ and have received of his marvelous power in my life. But it is even more important for you to know that you, too, can see him as I have seen him; that you, too, can talk with him as I have; and that you, too, can obtain his mighty power to help you accomplish all he would have you do." (See 1 Nephi 10:17, 19.)

What an electrifying, soul-transforming thought that was to me! It has continued to be the mainspring of my spiritual motivation and the greatest idea planted in my heart through the restored gospel.

THE TERRIBLE ACHE IN MY HEART LEFT ME

LOA M. RICHIE
Provo, Utah

Perhaps it was because I was born in a Latter-day Saint home to parents who were staunch in serving the Lord and in keeping the Lord's commandments that I grew up with great faith in my Father in Heaven and in His great love for me. For this reason I found myself often in a secluded place praying and talking to the Lord and thanking him for his many blessings to me and praying for continued guidance through each day.

I fell in love with a fine man, and we were married in the Salt Lake Temple. We were blessed with wonderful children. Then our seven-year-old son died suddenly and without warning. His death being so unnecessary, my husband and I were in no way prepared for such physical and mental and spiritual suffering and trauma. I lost all interest in living. I actually prayed sincerely to the Lord to allow me to die.

One day while I was busy in the kitchen, sorrowing over the loss of our seven-year-old son and wanting to be with him, it was as if someone spoke to me very clearly and told me that the devil was seeking to destroy me. I was told clearly to read the Book of Mormon and in this way I would receive much peace and comfort and also understanding pertaining to life and death. I did get my Book of Mormon off the shelf and I did read it. I carried it with me day and night and read it continually. When I slept, I kept the book under my pillow, so when my eyes were open in the night the book was at my disposal.

I can testify that I did receive peace and comfort by reading the Book of Mormon. It was at this time that I found out the real truthfulness of the Book of Mormon. My soul did rejoice because of the understanding and peace I received and still do receive in reading the Book of Mormon.

At the time our son died, I wanted so much to know about the spirit world, and I seemed to find nourishment for my spirit all through the Book of Mormon. When I came to Alma 40:11, where it says, "The spirits of all men, as soon as they are departed from this mortal body, . . . are taken home to that God who gave them life," I read the verse over and over, desiring to know more. My husband and I wanted to gain every assurance we could that we would be with our son again. He was an anchor in heaven to us.

My spirit was hungry, and my heart ached and pained more than can be described, and I kept reading the Book of Mormon. My spirit was greatly comforted as I read 3 Nephi, especially chapter 17, verse 20. Well, I read in verse 20 where Jesus spoke to the people and said, "Blessed are ye because of your faith. And now behold, my joy is full." When He had said these words, He wept—*and I wept too.* Then Jesus took the little children one by one and blessed them and prayed unto the Father for them.

I knew then as I know now that Christ's love for us is even greater than we can comprehend. I then knew Christ loved us and would guide us through. I had not read the Book of Mormon until that cold dreary day in February 1940 when I was instructed to do this. I have testified to my children that at the time I felt it was the Holy Ghost who instructed me to do this and it was loud and clear to me. I feasted on the Book of Mormon and it fed my spirit, and my testimony grew, and I felt a love in my heart for everyone. I missed our son—but the terrible ache in my heart left me.

I Tried to Break the Spell but Could Not Do It

Charles Randall Paul
Charleroi, Belgium

When I was fifteen, after reading the Book of Mormon, I kneeled, squeezed my eyes, my brain, and my spirit real hard, and nothing came out! The book had seemed "good," and "too complex for an unlearned kid to write," and even "as uplifting as the Bible," but there was no burning bush in the bedroom. The experience was, however, satisfying enough to allow me to go on faith: I *wanted* it to be true. That is, after all, the real test down here. Befogged in mortal amnesia, we search for what we want to be true while God observes. There is rarely overwhelming evidence for anything. I do mean anything.

Next step came at Brigham Young University in my freshman Book of Mormon class with Reid Bankhead. "It's what the book says that counts!" Those were his watch words. Bless him for making us answer questions with literal quotations from the book. The gospel is illuminated in the Book of Mormon better than in any other scripture. The doctrine on the Atonement came to me with the force of burning truth as I studied the book in my dorm at Helaman Halls. There were days when I would leave Bankhead's class "in love"—clicking my heels and dancing in the quad. What beauty and simplicity! What depth and reach! The gospel is true; that is, the doctrine of Christ, Immanuel, is true. I felt it deeply as the warmth of the Spirit covered me with confirmation. I didn't agree with Bankhead's politics (too black and white for me), but he's got to be up there with Parley P. Pratt when it comes to Book of Mormon heroes in this dispensation.

Then I went to France on my mission. I had been out just over two years. In a little apartment in an attic on a dirty street in Charleroi, Belgium, I sat reading in Helaman one Saturday night in 1965. As I pondered the passage, of a sudden, I was aware that *I knew* what I was reading actually occurred in ancient times. I felt as if my mind had left my body and was observing me holding the open book in my hands. An inner, quiet, joy surged as I knew, in an epistemological sense, *knew* that I was holding the Book of Books for our times. I knew that it was really of God and from God as well as I knew that I was holding it in my hands. I clutched it tighter to see if the physical pressure could outweigh the spiritual pressure. Like pinching myself to wake from a dream, I tried to break the spell but could not do it. To this day I feel compelled, almost like the Three Witnesses, to share with others these experiences with the book that has been a keystone to *my* religion for sure.

It Has Demanded a Pilgrimage of the Mind and Heart

David J. Whittaker
Yreka, California

When I was a sophomore in high school, my family lived about twenty-five miles from the town in which my school was located. This meant a long bus ride to and from school each day, a ride made even longer because of all the stops along the way. This was not too tiresome for me; the ride was through a scenic canyon, and there was always friendly conversation with fellow students. The only real problem came because of my participation in high school athletics — particularly basketball — which required after school practices and necessitated some creativity in getting home in the evenings.

There was the Greyhound bus, but it cost money, and it would only drop me off on the major highway about one mile away from my hometown. In the winter months this was particularly troublesome, but it did prevent hitchhiking, an alternative my parents forbade.

Fortunately my father was the branch president of our local Latter-day Saint congregation, and our chapel was near the high school. For a variety of reasons, the chapel proved to be a convenient rendezvous during the week. It was while walking to the chapel one evening following a basketball practice that I experienced my first and most powerful spiritual confirmation about the Book of Mormon.

Walking from the gym to our chapel covered about a quarter of a mile. Leaving the locker room, I walked across the south end of the football field, across a segment of the track, up a slight incline to a cement walk, then across a street and on to the chapel lawn. It was between the football field and the street that I experienced what I describe as an overwhelming spiritual presence that conveyed to my heart and mind that the Book of Mormon was a true record of Christ and his prophets and that this volume was exactly what Joseph Smith claimed it was. I saw no lights, no personages, heard no audible sounds, but felt a strong presence external to myself. I date my own testimony of the Book of Mormon from this experience in 1960.

I have reflected on this singular experience many times. It has both comforted and afflicted me in the years since. For one thing, I had not read the Book of Mormon either seriously or prayerfully prior to this experience. While my parents had no doubt used its stories in family home evening settings, and surely my Sunday School and priesthood teachers had also exposed me to its messages, I had not personally or substantially studied its contents. While my subsequent scholarly and devotional time with the volume have deepened and enlarged my testimony of its contents and messages, I truly had not begun my spiritual quest in the usual way.

I also discovered that, at least for me, there was a profound difference between knowing something is true and knowing what it means. Thus I have never doubted the truthfulness of the Book of Mormon, but I will spend my lifetime trying to grasp its meaning, trying to understand its message. While this has provided a great comfort to me spiritually, I am also afflicted by knowing that this is not enough. I must continually search and probe its contents for its meaning. For me this has meant surety on the foundational level of faith, but it has demanded a pilgrimage of the mind and the heart as I seek the deeper import and application to my personal life.

For many of my friends the process was somewhat reversed. Their testimony of the Book of Mormon came only after long and hard searching and prayer. For them the spiritual experience was confirmation; for me it was more origination, beginning my quest, as it were, with what is usually thought to come only at the end.

I do not know why it came this way to me. I do not think I was especially worthy or spiritual. In fact, I was really neither at that age. And the Lord must have known that I would not always sustain a life worthy of such an experience. Yet it was real, and it continues to sustain and enlighten my religious pilgrimage. For this alone, I will always be grateful.

I Felt Discernible Peace Fill My Body

Kenneth W. Godfrey
Tampa, Florida

There were very few books in our four-room house east of the railroad tracks on the north end of a twelve-acre farm. One volume we did have was George Reynolds' *The Story of the*

Book of Mormon, first published in 1888. In about 1940, while still a young boy, I picked it up one winter day. As the snow fell outside, I sat on a crimson-flowered couch next to a coal heater and encountered Nephi for the first time. A man of heroic proportions, Nephi lived a life, it seemed to me, that equaled that of Alexander the Great, Plato, Genghis Khan, or George Washington.

After finishing Reynolds I decided to read the Book of Mormon itself and began, like millions of others, with 1 Nephi. Though I was young, this book caused questions to rush into my mind. How could Laman and Lemuel continue to reject God after having been visited by an angel? Why did God require Nephi to cut off Laban's head? (At the time I could not decapitate a chicken at my father's request.) How could the untrained Nephi build a boat? (I was unable to construct a fence that looked decent, and the model airplane, a P-38, that I had tried to put together, looked like it had already been in too many battles with a German Messerschmitt or a Japanese Zero.)

Then I encountered 2 Nephi and Isaiah, and my questions were forgotten as I stopped reading and thought about the cows I had to milk, sports, and my homework. Over the next few years, I heard in both church meetings and Sunday School classes about other Book of Mormon heroes, such as Enos, Alma, General Moroni, Mormon, and Moroni. I even started to read the book again a few times. But there was always the impenetrable wall of 2 Nephi and the long quotations from Isaiah, and my reading would cease. Still I knew there was something extraordinary about the Book of Mormon. I had heard President Heber J. Grant say that Nephi was one of his heroes. So even though I was not reading it very often, it was still becoming part of my life, thoughts, and vocabulary.

I knew, for example, that Nephi was "born of goodly parents" (1 Nephi 1:1), that "men are, that they might have joy" (2 Nephi 2:25), that there "must needs be, that there is an opposition in all things" (v. 11), and that Nephi once said, "I will go and do the things which the Lord hath commanded, for I know that the Lord giveth no commandments unto the children of men, save he shall prepare a way for them that they may accomplish the thing which he commandeth them" (1 Nephi 3:7). I continued to be amazed each time I was told, which was often, that Enos had prayed all day and all night, because I did not see how that was possible, especially when it was all I could do to pray for two or three minutes. Moreover, I was also learning that if you skipped 2 Nephi there were other good parts to the Book of Mormon.

One Sabbath morning in 1953 (it seems now like it was in August) I was sitting at the sacrament table listening to the bishop give announcements, when suddenly he said, "We have just received word from the First Presidency that one boy in each ward, each year, will be allowed to go on a mission." I had been preparing to go into the service to fight in the Korean War, and even though I had always wanted to serve a mission and was worthy to do so, I had for some time believed my dream would not come true. But when the bishop made that announcement, I knew that I would be the young man selected to represent our ward that year. The following Thursday night, the bishop knocked on our front door, was invited in by my parents, and asked if I would be willing to accept a mission call. He could not have known in full the surge of joy that rushed through my body as I excitedly told him I would gladly accept. Unknown to me, my father spent much time on his knees in the barn that night pleading with the Lord to open up the way so that he could support me financially the two years I would be gone. I subsequently continued to work for the Union Pacific railroad, the pay from which enabled me to purchase two cows, which I gave to Dad. My wages also paid for my initial mission expenses, helping somewhat to answer his prayer.

Knowing that I would be required as a missionary to know what was in the Book of Mormon, I began seriously to study that volume of scripture, as well as the New Testament. This time I forced myself through the Isaiah passages and the allegory of Zenos and was thrilled by the wars, the stratagems, the victories, and the defeats found in the books of Mosiah and Alma. Samuel the Lamanite was added to my list of heroes, and the visit of the resurrected Savior to the Nephites spurred me on to read the tragic ending of that once faithful people.

While sitting in the mission home in Salt Lake City, I was listening one afternoon to Brigham Young University Professor Lynn McKinley, in his deep voice and with great feeling, speak about the Book of Mormon. As he concluded his talk he began to tell us how terribly important it was for all of us, individually, to obtain a testimony of the book's truthfulness. I realized that while I had read the book and believed that it was true, I did not yet have a sure witness, and I began to pray even as he ended his discourse. There came that moment to my soul a powerful, peaceful feeling accompanied by a quiet, almost imperceptible voice declaring that the Book of Mormon was true. All uncertainty fled; only assurance remained. That night, pondering the events of the day, I was impressed with how quickly my prayer of belief had been answered. I did not know then why a testimony had come so soon.

Upon my arrival in the Southern States Mission, I was assigned to labor in Tampa, Florida. My first companion was a recently discharged Marine who had been on his mission for only six months. Growing up, he had not been active in the Church but had cared more about cars, girls, and "good times." While he was engaged in a terrible battle in Korea's capital city, his sergeant, who was like a father to him, died in his arms. There quickly followed a change in my new companion's feelings and his life-style. He became active in the Church, and following his discharge he immediately came on a mission. He knew little about the gospel, less about the scriptures, and almost nothing about the history of the Church. I was his first junior companion, and at one of the first doors we knocked on my first day of tracting, we were met by a friendly, warm man who excitedly invited us into his home. I was amazed at how easy missionary work was and how ready people were to listen to our message. It was then that the man began to tell us that he knew all about Mormonism, its history, and the Book of Mormon. He asked us if we knew that Joseph Smith had placed a stone in a black hat which he pulled over his eyes as he translated the golden plates. He also declared that the Prophet placed in the Book of Mormon verses he had copied from the King James Bible, that the Book of Mormon also had excerpts from Shakespeare on its pages, and that it tried to answer every major controversy in the Prophet's own nineteenth-century religious world. Concluding, he asked, "What do you think of your prophet and his divine book now?"

I looked at my senior companion, anticipating answers that would utterly destroy our eager opponent. While still waiting, I heard him say, "Elder Godfrey, you grew up in the Church, you have been active all your life, you listened to all the lessons you were taught"—all of which was mostly true—"you answer the man!" A frightening, stunned feeling burst through my being. Then I heard myself say, "I don't know the answers to all your questions, but I have read the Book of Mormon. I know that what it teaches brings people closer to Christ and inspires them to both do good and be good; and what is more important right now is that I was told by the Holy Ghost, just a little more than a week ago, that the Book of Mormon is true. Your last question was, 'What do you think of your book now?' And my answer is, I know it is the word of God, and that it was translated by the gift and power of God, and the translation is correct." I felt a discernible peace fill my whole body as I said those words, peace accompanied by an assurance that I had just spoken the truth.

That night before going to sleep I contemplated the day's events. I knew why I had been given a testimony of the Book of Mormon so quickly, but I vowed that in the future I would know more about what was in that second witness for Christ, as well as more about its translation and the Church's history. Since then I have learned that if one has to choose, knowing that it is true is perhaps better than knowing how many times it mentions Christ, or how many examples of chiasmus are contained within its covers, or just which scribe wrote which part, or exactly what has been said about its translation.

While serving on my two-year mission, I was able to read the Book of Mormon seven times. Upon my return I took a Book of Mormon course at the Logan Institute of Religion, in which we studied that volume verse by verse. It was the spring quarter, and we were covering the last third of the book, which included the visit of Christ to the Nephites following his death and resurrection. I was struck with the concern He had for each person as He invited them all to feel his wounds. It impressed me that He did not have Nephi examine the marks on His body and then testify to the group what he had felt, nor did He encourage only the twelve disciples to do so. Rather, He took the time for each person to come forward and learn for himself or herself, until over twenty-five hundred people had done so.

Upon moving to Southern California, I was asked to teach for the Brigham Young University Department of Continuing Education a course titled "How to Teach the Book of Mormon." First, I tried to motivate the adults to read it, believing that once a person seriously begins to study its pages, a new love will have been found. Second, systematically I called attention to some of its major teachings with respect to the Fall, the Atonement, justice, mercy, patience, love, opposition, joy, and the factors that figure in the fall of civilizations. I then read its promise that all can know, if they will ask in faith, that the book is true. One ninety-two-year-old student had never petitioned God before regarding the Book of Mormon. After class one night, she retired to her apartment and, kneeling alone, put Moroni's promise to the test. Choked with emotion, she told the class the next week that her prayers had immediately been answered! Lamenting, she cried, "Why did I not ask sooner, because the joy I feel I have not felt before." The Book of Mormon, I found, as thousands had found before me, causes people's lives to change. They become more like Christ in their thoughts, feelings, actions, and speech.

I have thought often of the experience described in Third Nephi when the resurrected Christ visited the Nephites, instructed them, blessed them, and was about to depart for the night when He saw that the people "were in tears, and did look steadfastly upon him as if they would ask him to tarry a little longer with them." (3 Nephi 17:5.) Sometimes Latter-day Saints are taught to fear the Judgment and to look to that event with fear and trepidation. Yet the Nephites did not fear the "keeper of the gate"; rather, they desired to remain with Him longer.

My experience with the Book of Mormon has been a steady, simple friendship, never accompanied by angels, visions, or sudden dramatic events. Rather, it has kindled the gentle warmth of the fire of peace, the still small voice conveying love, and the feeling within that truth is quietly nestled on its pages. It has given me the deep impression that prophets of God inscribed scripture on plates of gold for a latter-day prophet to bring forth, and this scripture helps all peoples more surely walk on the narrow path at whose end stands a gate guarded by a keeper whose face I one day hope to see with pleasure.

I Brought It to My Father, with a Burning in My Heart

Catherine Weir
Footscray, Victoria, Australia

I was baptized into The Church of Jesus Christ of Latter-day Saints when I was eight years of age, in Glasgow, Scotland. My father had been told by his friends about the missionaries from The Church of Jesus Christ of Latter-day Saints, whom you could not prove wrong. "Send them around to my place, and I'll soon prove them wrong," boasted Dad. But Dad just could not prove them wrong, so he joined the Church when I was only five years old.

Not long after my baptism, when I was still eight years old, we left Scotland by ship to come to Australia to live, my parents and six children. Dad stayed active in the Church for about two years in Australia and so did the rest of my family, until we went to live in Benalla, a little country town in which there was no branch of the Church. The nearest branch was twenty-five miles away in Wangaratta. We attended that branch regularly, until, after he broke the Word of Wisdom, Dad's faith seemed to peter out. We all stopped attending church when Dad did, as he was our strength in the family as far as testimonies went.

I started attending different churches within the next five years or so. I went to the Presbyterian church and the Salvation Army, but finally when I was fifteen years old I decided to settle down in the Methodist church because they had a good youth club. One day while conversing with my Methodist minister, I asked him what church was true. "All churches are true," he tried to convince me. It just didn't make sense to me. How can the truth contradict itself? and I had been taught contradicting concepts in each church.

When I got home, I told my father about my conversation with my minister. Dad's response caught me by surprise: "Go and get me the Book of Mormon, and I'll show you what church it true." We had not had contact with the LDS church for about five years. Since we had changed addresses five times, we could have thrown the Book of Mormon away. Not knowing where to begin my search, I said a silent prayer: "Dear Heavenly Father, if this is the true church, please help me find the Book of Mormon. In the name of Jesus Christ. Amen."

The first place I looked I found it and took it to my father with a burning in my heart. I did not know what burnings in your heart meant at that stage. As I presented this book to my father, he acted strangely, refusing to let me have the book, saying, "No, it may be too hard for you to live up to. What you do not know you cannot be held responsible for." He held fast to the book, preventing me even from touching it anymore.

"Please, Dad," I begged, "you can't stop now. You have aroused my interest too much." So Dad opened the Book of Mormon at the promise where God tells you that if you read the book with a sincere heart, with real intent, having faith in Christ, he will manifest the truth of it unto you by the power of the Holy Ghost. (See Moroni 10:4.)

Being a very inquisitive fifteen-year-old, I decided, "Right, so I am going to put this promise to the test." I started doing as the promise instructed, reading and praying to find out if the Book of Mormon was true.

Within two weeks, missionaries from The Church of Jesus Christ of Latter-day Saints came knocking on my door, though this was the first time in five years we had had any contact with the Church. They told me where and when they held their meetings, inviting me to come along. I accepted their invitation, and as I sat through their meeting (which was held in a small recreation hall because they did not have a chapel built in the Footscray area at that time, about 1961), I realized I had never felt the Holy Ghost's presence so strongly in any of the other churches I had attended. I felt that the Lord was close to me within this church. I knew this was where the Lord wanted me to be. I knew this was His true church. This knowledge just increased as years went by and so did the feeling of getting closer to our Lord, till, as years have gone by, this closeness has brought unspeakable joy, which makes me desire never to leave His side.

The missionary who found me when I was fifteen years old told me later that he and his companion were not supposed to be knocking on my street, but he had felt motivated by the Spirit to come and knock on my door. I believe they were sent by God as an answer to my prayers.

The Loss of That Book Is
Bearable: It Was Only a Catalyst
W. Bryan Stout
Linares, Chile

When I entered the Language Training Mission to prepare to serve a mission in Chile in 1975, my testimony was young and tender—the only thing I could say I knew with certainty was that God lived and answered prayers. I spent my first four months in the mission field as junior companion to Robert Duane Lyman, who suggested I mark the scriptures with thirteen colors of pencils, one for each Article of Faith, using whatever color would be most appropriate to the passage. That idea intrigued me, and in my second city I decided to use that approach with the Book of Mormon.

For the purpose of my study, I expanded the scope of each color I used: With the first article of faith I included all discussion of the nature of any member of the Godhead; with the second, any discussion of sin or free agency; with the fourth, the sacrament and enduring to the end with the first principles of the gospel; with the thirteenth, doctrines about righteousness and commandments; and so on.

At the beginning, my study was no different from most previous occasions when I had read the scriptures. But something special started happening at 1 Nephi 10:17–22. I found myself using about half my pencils for this passage and felt the quiet but strong witness of the Spirit to its truthfulness, all the more penetrating on this occasion when I was aware of all the doctrine being powerfully taught.

This experience became common. Again and again I was impressed with the conciseness, clarity, and boldness the Book of Mormon used in proclaiming its doctrine. Again and again the Spirit both bore witness to the truth and helped me see the depth and power lying behind the simple words. As the weeks went by, I benefited from this study in a variety of ways.

Not only was I uplifted personally, but I was able to bear a strong, glad testimony to the restored gospel.

From this study I came to love Isaiah. For the first time I was able to understand his message and appreciate the beauty of his expression. The Book of Mormon narrative became more alive to me than ever before. When I read of Nephi frankly forgiving his brother for leaving him in the wilderness to die, I wept and thought of the anguish Nephi and Lehi must have felt as Laman and Lemuel vacillated between rebellion and repentance and finally rebelled for life. When the combined Nephite and Lamanite army decisively beat the Gadianton robbers, I wept again, sharing the people's joy in their deliverance.

I was liberal in my underlining, and my use of different colors helped me notice things I would probably have missed otherwise. I used a purple pencil for the twelfth article of faith and church-state relations; there was more purple in Mosiah than in the rest of the Book of Mormon combined. I saw that government was a central theme of Mosiah, starting with the good example of King Benjamin and the bad example of King Noah and finishing with the sermons of Alma the Elder and King Mosiah explaining principles of good government.

I used a sandy color for the tenth article of faith and the role of God in history, and from its use I noticed a sandwich structure to the Book of Mormon: most of the quotations from the Old Testament and nearly all the prophecies about the last days occur either at the beginning in the small plates of Nephi or at the end of the book, starting with the appearance of Jesus Christ. The large central portion is filled mainly with detailed narrative and gospel sermons. I also saw that Moroni, the book's last author, deliberately echoed themes stated by the first author, Nephi, such as speaking to us from the dust and testifying to us at the judgment bar of God.

The biggest benefit I received was a deeper communion with the Spirit than I ever had before. King Benjamin's discourse on the mission of Christ, service, and spiritual rebirth exulted me and gave me more joy in life than any other passage.

With Ether 12:4 I had an experience similar to the one Joseph Smith had with James 1:5. The idea that hope is the anchor to our souls, which leads us to abound in good works entered "with great force into every feeling of my heart." Ever since then, when it has been my responsibility to motivate others, I have tried to do it with hope, not guilt.

And so a suggestion from my first companion led me to the solid core of my testimony and helped build the spiritual foundation for the rest of my life. This method of multiple colors isn't for everyone: Another missionary I told my experience to tried it but gave it up as too involved. But it worked for me and taught me things I might not have learned in any other way.

In the years since my mission, that rainbow-colored copy of the Book of Mormon became a treasured possession and personal reference work. Unfortunately, I no longer have it. While I was in graduate school and inside the institute building helping at a function, someone passing through the parking lot stole my backpack out of an automobile. There is a poignant irony in that a heavily marked Spanish Book of Mormon was probably the most useless item in the pack to the thief, but it was the only irreplaceable item to me. The loss of that book is bearable, though, for it was only a catalyst in obtaining the real treasure. I still have a strong testimony of Christ and his gospel, and I am still getting insight from the Book of Mormon and the other scriptures.

THE BOOK IS FULL OF RICHNESS, LIKE FLOWERS IN CRANNIED WALLS

CLAUDIA L. BUSHMAN
Newark, Delaware

The truth is that I don't much like the Book of Mormon. Reading it is tantalizing and disturbing because so much has been left out. If I had stood beside Nephi or Mormon with a stylus and some sheets of gold, the book would have told a different story, full of anecdotes of real life in Zarahemla, with full descriptions of houses, fashion, and the educational system. I would have described cities, sports, and commerce. I would have talked about family life. I certainly would have said something about the invisible and silent majority. Where are the women's pages of the Book of Mormon? Were they abridged out, or did they just never exist?

Then I don't like the people. A superrighteous and superior younger brother is enough to drive anyone to sin, and controlling the record as he does, he will not present his siblings in a very good light. And I have never been sympathetic to the elevation of overnight repenters like Alma. The return of the prodigal son is certainly cause for rejoicing, but he should come in below those who have been continually faithful, certainly not raised to their head. If those who have experienced evil can really be better than those who have always been good, let's hear it in some official way and incorporate it into the system. Helaman's stripling warriors make me very sad because their innocent faith seems wrongly placed. All men will die, and many of the righteous will die battling those who are equally righteous. The Book of Mormon is full of firm-jawed, single-minded, unsympathetic people.

Then the structure is so very complex, a compilation of fragments and diverse texts, all run together in a strange way. The people traverse a bleak landscape, traveling and fighting, with little sense of progress. They sin and repent, sin and repent against an ever repeated chorus—be good, be good.

But when I read the Book of Mormon, the first verse always seems heavy with wisdom, direction, meaning. Why have I never noticed this before, I wonder. This verse should be memorized, used as the basis of a talk, worked into a sampler. And the book is full of richness, like the golden eyes of toads or flowers in crannied walls. Hundreds of pages of small verses full of hidden jewels.

IT HAS OPENED MY HEART WIDER TO EXPERIENCE HIS LOVE

Robert A. Rees
Los Angeles, California

I love the Book of Mormon. I have since the first day I heard about it when I was ten years old. I learned about the Book of Mormon from my father, who had just returned from the second world war. Before going into the service he had been miraculously converted to the gospel through a priesthood blessing that brought him back from the brink of death. Perhaps it was a combination of youthful openness and a gift of faith, but when I heard the story of the coming forth of the Book of Mormon, I was blessed at that moment to know that what I was hearing was true. Somehow I just knew it. That witness has never left me, even though as a scholar and thinker I have wrestled with numerous questions or "problems" relating to the book.

I love to read the Book of Mormon. It is an inviting book, one that rewards the frequent and careful reader. My experience with it over the years has been the same as with the other standard works: the more I read them, the more riches they yield. Thoughtful, sensitive reading of the Book of Mormon reveals the depth, complexity, and subtlety of this great second testament of Christ. Each time I read it, I see things I have never seen before. One of the reasons for this is that I come back to the book a different person from the one I was on the previous reading. Not only have I had more experiences with the Spirit since the last reading but I have struggled more with my own weaknesses and transgressions, have suffered the pain of trying to be a better husband and father, and have faced the challenge of being a better Christian and, in whatever church calling I have, a better steward.

I love to read the Book of Mormon because as I do, the Spirit bears witness to me that what I am reading is true, and this strengthens my bond to God. I have thought often about why the Lord has commanded us to read the scriptures. I am convinced that the chief reason is that as we read about the experiences of actual men and women and see how God acted in their lives, we are convinced that he can act is our lives as well. Further, as the Holy Ghost reveals to our hearts and minds the truth of what we are reading, we experience the love of God in a profound way. In fact, one might say that the whole purpose of the gospel and the Church is to provide us with opportunities to experience God's love personally and to share that love with others. In this way, we come to experience, as the angel testified to Nephi, "the love of God, which sheddeth itself abroad in the hearts of the children of men" and to know that "it is the most desirable above all things. . . . Yea, and the most joyous to the soul." (1 Nephi 11:22–23.) The revelation of that love is available through reading the Book of Mormon. I have felt it frequently, deeply, and richly.

I love to study the Book of Mormon. I make a distinction between reading and studying. Generally, we read the Book of Mormon for inspiration and comfort, but we study it to gain understanding. One of the reasons why I love to study the Book of Mormon is that through serious, thoughtful study I am able to test the book's true mettle.

I first learned how to study the Book of Mormon when I was a student at Brigham Young University. There, under the tutelage of such great teachers as Robert Thomas, Truman Madsen, Hugh Nibley, Reid Bankhead, Glen Pearson, and others, I began a serious study of the Book of Mormon and learned to respect its toughness.

From Robert Thomas, who awakened me both intellectually and spiritually, I first gained an appreciation for the literary qualities of the Book of Mormon. Bob had written his undergraduate thesis at Reed College on the parallels between biblical poetic style and that of the Book of Mormon, and as a budding literary scholar I was intrigued by his insights. Hugh Nibley taught me how to consider the ancient antecedents of

the book and how to read carefully to discover the book's
message for our dispensation. Truman Madsen taught me how
to connect the book's great messages with the rich philosophical, spiritual, and historical truths in other religions and traditions. In Reid Bankhead's class on Jesus the Christ I understood for the first time what the atonement of Christ meant to
me personally. That experience was enhanced by Brother Bankhead's showing me how the Book of Mormon enlightens our
understanding of the Atonement. Brother Pearson taught me
that the Book of Mormon was the key to conversion, a lesson
I was to apply many times as a missionary.

In graduate school I studied literary theory and criticism,
and what I learned gave me a new appreciation for the linguistic
complexity and literary beauty of the record of Nephi. The
more I learned about the integrity of a literary text, the more
I was convinced that no one living in 1830 could have written
the Book of Mormon. In fact, I am convinced that all the scholars
and theologians in the world in 1830, working with all the
known texts and reference materials, could not have written
what was translated from the brass plates. The intricacies of
the various literary styles, the complicated narrative, and especially the spiritual insights all suggest a time and a people
that neither Joseph Smith nor any of his contemporaries could
have invented. There are just too many places where the authenticity of the text rings true.

It is in the details that any text has its greatest test, and it
is in the details of the Book of Mormon that I often find things
that give intellectual and rational support to the spiritual witness I have received. For example, when Nephi tells his people
to let their souls "delight in fatness" (2 Nephi 9:51), I am
convinced that this is not a metaphorical expression that Joseph
Smith or his contemporaries might have used. It is one expression among many in the Book of Mormon that to my mind
could not have been invented or faked.

I love to teach the Book of Mormon. Over the years I have
had many opportunities to teach it both formally and infor-

mally. I have taught it as a Primary, Sunday School, and Young Men's teacher; I have taught it in various priesthood quorums; and I have taught it as a seminary and institute teacher. In such classes I have taken pleasure in opening the pages of the Book of Mormon to my students and in turn having them enlighten my understanding.

As a father it has been my privilege to teach the Book of Mormon to my children and to testify of its truth to them. One of my greatest joys has been to see my children grow up with their own testimonies of the Book of Mormon and to see them share those testimonies with others through missionary work, teaching in the Church, and testifying to friends and acquaintances. In this way the light of this great book is passed from generation to generation and to the wider world.

As the bishop of a singles ward for the past three years, I have had many occasions to teach the truths of the Book of Mormon to members of my congregation. I have found it a great resource for touching the lives of others and challenging them to greater faithfulness. For example, not long ago I was counseling a young man who had been involved in a series of sexual transgressions. He was not convinced that what he had done was particularly wrong or that it would have serious consequences in his life. As I was trying to convince him of the error of his ways and help him come to a place of repentance, I remembered Alma's words to his son Corianton. Turning to Alma 39 through 42, I read Alma's counsel to Corianton and concluded with the words of this faithful father to his errant son: "Behold, I say unto you, wickedness never was happiness." (Alma 41:10.)

I love to teach the Book of Mormon because it is a very teachable book. Since it deals with the fundamental problems of human relationships, the archetypal conflict between good and evil, and the eternal struggle between our wills and God's, it provides many great lessons that can inspire faithfulness. Like all great literature, it allows us to identify imaginatively with the characters who inhabit its pages. Further, since it was written expressly for our day, as teachers we are able to relate its principles to the real world around us. Like Nephi, we are able to "liken all scriptures unto us, that it might be for our profit and learning." (1 Nephi 19:23.)

I love to testify of the Book of Mormon. Knowing how much joy the book has brought me, I have sought for opportunities to tell others about its truths. When I was a young missionary, it gave me a thrill to testify to the people I met in cities and towns in the Midwest of the Lord's work among the ancient Americans. The very first person I taught on my first day of tracting on a cold January day in 1956 in Kankakee, Illinois, I testified to about the truth of the Restoration, including the coming forth of the Book of Mormon. She received a witness through my humble testimony that I spoke the truth and was converted to the Church that day. Since then I have testified to thousands of the truth of this second witness of Jesus Christ and have felt that exquisite joy that comes when one is an instrument in bringing another to Christ.

I have had many conversations with others about the Book of Mormon. Several of these stand out in my memory. I have had the privilege for the past eight years of working with Dr. Norman Cousins in organizing a series of exchanges between writers from China and the United States. This has given me a rare opportunity of knowing some of the outstanding writers from both countries. At one conference in Los Angeles, I was having a conversation with the American writer Kurt Vonnegut. When he found out I was a Mormon, he asked me if I really believed what the Church taught. I assured him that I did. He then asked me how I regarded the Book of Mormon. I told him I considered it an authentic record. He asked, "How can you believe something like that?" My response was the same as that which I have given to my students at the university over the years: "If I am intellectually and spiritually honest with myself, I have to say that the spiritual conviction I receive when reading the Book of Mormon is among the truest experiences I have ever had."

I had a similar discussion with the poet Allen Ginsberg in Souzhou, China. We were at a gathering of writers one evening, and the discussion somehow turned to religion. When Allen asked what I believed, I gave him a brief summary of our teachings, including the story of the Book of Mormon. He asked incredulously, "This is actually believed?" I assured him that indeed it was and that I was one of the believers. Allen is a practicing Buddhist and has respect and tolerance for the beliefs of others, but this particular set of beliefs seemed to stretch the limits of his ecumenical spirit.

I also told my Chinese friends about the Book of Mormon and included copies of it in collections of American books that our delegation gave to the Chinese Writers' Association libraries in Beijing and Shanghai. On a trip to the Soviet Union, I gave a copy to a friend in Leningrad, and in Moscow I had an interesting conversation with a Russian associate who had been reading a copy of the Book of Mormon given him in December 1987 by my friend Gene Kovalenko. I have sent copies of the Book of Mormon to friends and associates, and my family has sent copies with our photograph and testimony to anonymous readers through the family to family Book of Mormon program.

I love the Book of Mormon most of all because it has led me to a fuller understanding of the life and mission of Jesus Christ and has opened my heart wider to experience His love. The Book of Mormon testifies of Christ from the very first chapter, where Lehi sees "One descending out of the midst of heaven [whose] luster was above that of the sun at noon-day" (1 Nephi 1:9), to the very last chapter, where Moroni says, "If ye by the grace of God are perfect in Christ, and deny not his power, then are ye sanctified in Christ by the grace of God, through the shedding of the blood of Christ, which is in the covenant of the Father unto the remission of your sins, that ye become holy, without spot" (Moroni 10:33). Through the many testimonies of Book of Mormon prophets and through Christ's own words to the Nephites, I have come to exclaim, as does

Nephi, "I glory in plainness; I glory in truth; I glory in *my* Jesus, for he hath redeemed my soul from hell." (2 Nephi 33:6; italics added.)

I love the Book of Mormon. And I love the Lord for sending it to bless our lives.

INDEX